C-3979 CAREER EXAMINATION SERIES

This is your
PASSBOOK for...

Geographic Information System Analyst

Test Preparation Study Guide
Questions & Answers

COPYRIGHT NOTICE

This book is SOLELY intended for, is sold ONLY to, and its use is RESTRICTED to individual, bona fide applicants or candidates who qualify by virtue of having seriously filed applications for appropriate license, certificate, professional and/or promotional advancement, higher school matriculation, scholarship, or other legitimate requirements of education and/or governmental authorities.

This book is NOT intended for use, class instruction, tutoring, training, duplication, copying, reprinting, excerption, or adaptation, etc., by:

1) Other publishers
2) Proprietors and/or Instructors of "Coaching" and/or Preparatory Courses
3) Personnel and/or Training Divisions of commercial, industrial, and governmental organizations
4) Schools, colleges, or universities and/or their departments and staffs, including teachers and other personnel
5) Testing Agencies or Bureaus
6) Study groups which seek by the purchase of a single volume to copy and/or duplicate and/or adapt this material for use by the group as a whole without having purchased individual volumes for each of the members of the group
7) Et al.

Such persons would be in violation of appropriate Federal and State statutes.

PROVISION OF LICENSING AGREEMENTS – Recognized educational, commercial, industrial, and governmental institutions and organizations, and others legitimately engaged in educational pursuits, including training, testing, and measurement activities, may address request for a licensing agreement to the copyright owners, who will determine whether, and under what conditions, including fees and charges, the materials in this book may be used them. In other words, a licensing facility exists for the legitimate use of the material in this book on other than an individual basis. However, it is asseverated and affirmed here that the material in this book CANNOT be used without the receipt of the express permission of such a licensing agreement from the Publishers. Inquiries re licensing should be addressed to the company, attention rights and permissions department.

All rights reserved, including the right of reproduction in whole or in part, in any form or by any means, electronic or mechanical, including photocopying, recording, or by any information storage and retrieval system, without permission in writing from the Publisher.

Copyright © 2025 by
National Learning Corporation

212 Michael Drive, Syosset, NY 11791
(516) 921-8888 • www.passbooks.com
E-mail: info@passbooks.com

PASSBOOK® SERIES

THE *PASSBOOK® SERIES* has been created to prepare applicants and candidates for the ultimate academic battlefield – the examination room.

At some time in our lives, each and every one of us may be required to take an examination – for validation, matriculation, admission, qualification, registration, certification, or licensure.

Based on the assumption that every applicant or candidate has met the basic formal educational standards, has taken the required number of courses, and read the necessary texts, the *PASSBOOK® SERIES* furnishes the one special preparation which may assure passing with confidence, instead of failing with insecurity. Examination questions – together with answers – are furnished as the basic vehicle for study so that the mysteries of the examination and its compounding difficulties may be eliminated or diminished by a sure method.

This book is meant to help you pass your examination provided that you qualify and are serious in your objective.

The entire field is reviewed through the huge store of content information which is succinctly presented through a provocative and challenging approach – the question-and-answer method.

A climate of success is established by furnishing the correct answers at the end of each test.

You soon learn to recognize types of questions, forms of questions, and patterns of questioning. You may even begin to anticipate expected outcomes.

You perceive that many questions are repeated or adapted so that you can gain acute insights, which may enable you to score many sure points.

You learn how to confront new questions, or types of questions, and to attack them confidently and work out the correct answers.

You note objectives and emphases, and recognize pitfalls and dangers, so that you may make positive educational adjustments.

Moreover, you are kept fully informed in relation to new concepts, methods, practices, and directions in the field.

You discover that you are actually taking the examination all the time: you are preparing for the examination by "taking" an examination, not by reading extraneous and/or supererogatory textbooks.

In short, this PASSBOOK®, used directedly, should be an important factor in helping you to pass your test.

GEOGRAPHIC INFORMATION SYSTEMS ANALYST

DUTIES:
A Geographic Information Systems Analyst develops and maintains end user applications in Geographic Information Systems Software in a client server environment; reviews work and information flow and determines end user requirements; writes and tests end user and data administration applications; works with data processing supervisor and staff to develop integrated enterprise Geographic Information Systems; writes design specifications for database tables and applications; designs detailed programs to add to or enhance database entries relating to their display, modifications and utilization; makes recommendations for data model improvements and changes through field observations; designs highly detailed programs within the guidelines of the GIS system administrator or data processing supervisor to enhance the display modification and utilization of database entries; codes programs and changes within the prescribed standard of documentation; installs and tests new versions of Geographic Information Systems software; evaluates software packages for compatibility; performs analyses and quality control of data conversions; creates and tests new data models, tables, symbol sets and data editing/integration routines; develops detailed user instructions and conducts user training; assists the operations staff in solving problems as they may occur during system development and operation.

TYPICAL WORK ACTIVITIES:
- Creates and maintains geographic data in geographic or database formats; updates geographic features using GIS software from electronic or paper sources such as service cards, lists, forms, shapefiles, maps, databases and GPS devices or files;
- Designs and implements cartographic projects and spatial analyses including address matching (geocoding); responds to map and data requests from County staff, officials and the public;
- Creates or customizes GIS interfaces in ArcPad Application Builder, ArcGIS Desktop, Arc Reader, ArcGIS Explorer, Google maps and similar interfaces and platforms;
- Designs and documents methodologies for data collection, maintenance and documentation projects including quality control plans; implements such projects under the supervision of the Department Director;
- Investigates and evaluates potential sources of data and assesses their quality, accuracy and completeness; designs processes to link databases and corresponding geographic features; meets with County staff to assess the usability of data sources for creating or updating GIS files;
- Assists Department Director in project design and management for large data and analysis Projects; Documents methodologies, processes and project operations; compiles electronic map and data catalogs; and creates and maintains metadata for GIS files;
- Designs and coordinates work done by a GIS Intern;
- Assists the Department Director in performing system-wide assessments and implementing new programs and procedures;
- May perform fieldwork to obtain and/or verify data.

SUBJECT OF EXAMINATION:
The written test is designed to evaluate knowledge, skills, and/or abilities in the following areas:
1. **Understanding and interpreting maps, aerial photography, survey data and other source material used in map construction** -These questions test for the ability to read, analyze and perform computations based on cartographic drawings, site plans, survey notes and mapping-related written presentations, and for knowledge of the terminology and principals involved in reading and working with aerial photographs, including scale conversion and focal point computations.
2. **Collection, analysis and presentation of data, including basic statistics** - These questions test for knowledge of the proper procedures and methods used to gather, evaluate, organize and present various types of technical data and information, and the fundamental concepts, terminology and computations involved in statistical analysis for cartographic and land use planning studies.
3. **Computer-assisted mapping, including geographic information system (GIS) applications** - These questions test for knowledge of the concepts, terminology, and proper procedures to use when creating and revising maps and site plans utilizing GIS and computerized mapping software.
4. **Principles of data bases for microcomputers** - These questions test for a basic background in the design and use of databases on microcomputers. They cover such topics as database terminology and concepts, analyzing a database project, planning the database, organizing the data, designing data entry forms, accessing and manipulating the data, generating reports, and performing backups.
5. **Geographic Information Systems (GIS), including data conversion, plotting, database construction, interactive editing and labeling** - These questions test for knowledge of GIS design features, global positioning systems, and the concepts, terminology and proper procedures to use when creating, producing and revising various types of maps and site plans using GIS and computerized mapping software.

HOW TO TAKE A TEST

I. YOU MUST PASS AN EXAMINATION

A. WHAT EVERY CANDIDATE SHOULD KNOW

Examination applicants often ask us for help in preparing for the written test. What can I study in advance? What kinds of questions will be asked? How will the test be given? How will the papers be graded?

As an applicant for a civil service examination, you may be wondering about some of these things. Our purpose here is to suggest effective methods of advance study and to describe civil service examinations.

Your chances for success on this examination can be increased if you know how to prepare. Those "pre-examination jitters" can be reduced if you know what to expect. You can even experience an adventure in good citizenship if you know why civil service exams are given.

B. WHY ARE CIVIL SERVICE EXAMINATIONS GIVEN?

Civil service examinations are important to you in two ways. As a citizen, you want public jobs filled by employees who know how to do their work. As a job seeker, you want a fair chance to compete for that job on an equal footing with other candidates. The best-known means of accomplishing this two-fold goal is the competitive examination.

Exams are widely publicized throughout the nation. They may be administered for jobs in federal, state, city, municipal, town or village governments or agencies.

Any citizen may apply, with some limitations, such as the age or residence of applicants. Your experience and education may be reviewed to see whether you meet the requirements for the particular examination. When these requirements exist, they are reasonable and applied consistently to all applicants. Thus, a competitive examination may cause you some uneasiness now, but it is your privilege and safeguard.

C. HOW ARE CIVIL SERVICE EXAMS DEVELOPED?

Examinations are carefully written by trained technicians who are specialists in the field known as "psychological measurement," in consultation with recognized authorities in the field of work that the test will cover. These experts recommend the subject matter areas or skills to be tested; only those knowledges or skills important to your success on the job are included. The most reliable books and source materials available are used as references. Together, the experts and technicians judge the difficulty level of the questions.

Test technicians know how to phrase questions so that the problem is clearly stated. Their ethics do not permit "trick" or "catch" questions. Questions may have been tried out on sample groups, or subjected to statistical analysis, to determine their usefulness.

Written tests are often used in combination with performance tests, ratings of training and experience, and oral interviews. All of these measures combine to form the best-known means of finding the right person for the right job.

II. HOW TO PASS THE WRITTEN TEST

A. NATURE OF THE EXAMINATION

To prepare intelligently for civil service examinations, you should know how they differ from school examinations you have taken. In school you were assigned certain definite pages to read or subjects to cover. The examination questions were quite detailed and usually emphasized memory. Civil service exams, on the other hand, try to discover your present ability to perform the duties of a position, plus your potentiality to learn these duties. In other words, a civil service exam attempts to predict how successful you will be. Questions cover such a broad area that they cannot be as minute and detailed as school exam questions.

In the public service similar kinds of work, or positions, are grouped together in one "class." This process is known as *position-classification*. All the positions in a class are paid according to the salary range for that class. One class title covers all of these positions, and they are all tested by the same examination.

B. FOUR BASIC STEPS

1) Study the announcement

How, then, can you know what subjects to study? Our best answer is: "Learn as much as possible about the class of positions for which you've applied." The exam will test the knowledge, skills and abilities needed to do the work.

Your most valuable source of information about the position you want is the official exam announcement. This announcement lists the training and experience qualifications. Check these standards and apply only if you come reasonably close to meeting them.

The brief description of the position in the examination announcement offers some clues to the subjects which will be tested. Think about the job itself. Review the duties in your mind. Can you perform them, or are there some in which you are rusty? Fill in the blank spots in your preparation.

Many jurisdictions preview the written test in the exam announcement by including a section called "Knowledge and Abilities Required," "Scope of the Examination," or some similar heading. Here you will find out specifically what fields will be tested.

2) Review your own background

Once you learn in general what the position is all about, and what you need to know to do the work, ask yourself which subjects you already know fairly well and which need improvement. You may wonder whether to concentrate on improving your strong areas or on building some background in your fields of weakness. When the announcement has specified "some knowledge" or "considerable knowledge," or has used adjectives like "beginning principles of..." or "advanced ... methods," you can get a clue as to the number and difficulty of questions to be asked in any given field. More questions, and hence broader coverage, would be included for those subjects which are more important in the work. Now weigh your strengths and weaknesses against the job requirements and prepare accordingly.

3) Determine the level of the position

Another way to tell how intensively you should prepare is to understand the level of the job for which you are applying. Is it the entering level? In other words, is this the position in which beginners in a field of work are hired? Or is it an intermediate or advanced level? Sometimes this is indicated by such words as "Junior" or "Senior" in the class title. Other jurisdictions use Roman numerals to designate the level – Clerk I, Clerk II, for example. The word "Supervisor" sometimes appears in the title. If the level is not indicated by the title, check the description of duties. Will you be working under very close supervision, or will you have responsibility for independent decisions in this work?

4) Choose appropriate study materials

Now that you know the subjects to be examined and the relative amount of each subject to be covered, you can choose suitable study materials. For beginning level jobs, or even advanced ones, if you have a pronounced weakness in some aspect of your training, read a modern, standard textbook in that field. Be sure it is up to date and has general coverage. Such books are normally available at your library, and the librarian will be glad to help you locate one. For entry-level positions, questions of appropriate difficulty are chosen – neither highly advanced questions, nor those too simple. Such questions require careful thought but not advanced training.

If the position for which you are applying is technical or advanced, you will read more advanced, specialized material. If you are already familiar with the basic principles of your field, elementary textbooks would waste your time. Concentrate on advanced textbooks and technical periodicals. Think through the concepts and review difficult problems in your field.

These are all general sources. You can get more ideas on your own initiative, following these leads. For example, training manuals and publications of the government agency which employs workers in your field can be useful, particularly for technical and professional positions. A letter or visit to the government department involved may result in more specific study suggestions, and certainly will provide you with a more definite idea of the exact nature of the position you are seeking.

III. KINDS OF TESTS

Tests are used for purposes other than measuring knowledge and ability to perform specified duties. For some positions, it is equally important to test ability to make adjustments to new situations or to profit from training. In others, basic mental abilities not dependent on information are essential. Questions which test these things may not appear as pertinent to the duties of the position as those which test for knowledge and information. Yet they are often highly important parts of a fair examination. For very general questions, it is almost impossible to help you direct your study efforts. What we can do is to point out some of the more common of these general abilities needed in public service positions and describe some typical questions.

1) General information

Broad, general information has been found useful for predicting job success in some kinds of work. This is tested in a variety of ways, from vocabulary lists to questions about current events. Basic background in some field of work, such as sociology or economics, may be sampled in a group of questions. Often these are principles which have become familiar to most persons through exposure rather than through formal training. It is difficult to advise you how to study for these questions; being alert to the world around you is our best suggestion.

2) Verbal ability

An example of an ability needed in many positions is verbal or language ability. Verbal ability is, in brief, the ability to use and understand words. Vocabulary and grammar tests are typical measures of this ability. Reading comprehension or paragraph interpretation questions are common in many kinds of civil service tests. You are given a paragraph of written material and asked to find its central meaning.

3) Numerical ability

Number skills can be tested by the familiar arithmetic problem, by checking paired lists of numbers to see which are alike and which are different, or by interpreting charts and graphs. In the latter test, a graph may be printed in the test booklet which you are asked to use as the basis for answering questions.

4) Observation

A popular test for law-enforcement positions is the observation test. A picture is shown to you for several minutes, then taken away. Questions about the picture test your ability to observe both details and larger elements.

5) Following directions

In many positions in the public service, the employee must be able to carry out written instructions dependably and accurately. You may be given a chart with several columns, each column listing a variety of information. The questions require you to carry out directions involving the information given in the chart.

6) Skills and aptitudes

Performance tests effectively measure some manual skills and aptitudes. When the skill is one in which you are trained, such as typing or shorthand, you can practice. These tests are often very much like those given in business school or high school courses. For many of the other skills and aptitudes, however, no short-time preparation can be made. Skills and abilities natural to you or that you have developed throughout your lifetime are being tested.

Many of the general questions just described provide all the data needed to answer the questions and ask you to use your reasoning ability to find the answers. Your best preparation for these tests, as well as for tests of facts and ideas, is to be at your physical and mental best. You, no doubt, have your own methods of getting into an exam-taking mood and keeping "in shape." The next section lists some ideas on this subject.

IV. KINDS OF QUESTIONS

Only rarely is the "essay" question, which you answer in narrative form, used in civil service tests. Civil service tests are usually of the short-answer type. Full instructions for answering these questions will be given to you at the examination. But in case this is your first experience with short-answer questions and separate answer sheets, here is what you need to know:

1) Multiple-choice Questions

Most popular of the short-answer questions is the "multiple choice" or "best answer" question. It can be used, for example, to test for factual knowledge, ability to solve problems or judgment in meeting situations found at work.

A multiple-choice question is normally one of three types—
- It can begin with an incomplete statement followed by several possible endings. You are to find the one ending which *best* completes the statement, although some of the others may not be entirely wrong.
- It can also be a complete statement in the form of a question which is answered by choosing one of the statements listed.

- It can be in the form of a problem – again you select the best answer.

Here is an example of a multiple-choice question with a discussion which should give you some clues as to the method for choosing the right answer:

When an employee has a complaint about his assignment, the action which will *best* help him overcome his difficulty is to
- A. discuss his difficulty with his coworkers
- B. take the problem to the head of the organization
- C. take the problem to the person who gave him the assignment
- D. say nothing to anyone about his complaint

In answering this question, you should study each of the choices to find which is best. Consider choice "A" – Certainly an employee may discuss his complaint with fellow employees, but no change or improvement can result, and the complaint remains unresolved. Choice "B" is a poor choice since the head of the organization probably does not know what assignment you have been given, and taking your problem to him is known as "going over the head" of the supervisor. The supervisor, or person who made the assignment, is the person who can clarify it or correct any injustice. Choice "C" is, therefore, correct. To say nothing, as in choice "D," is unwise. Supervisors have and interest in knowing the problems employees are facing, and the employee is seeking a solution to his problem.

2) True/False Questions

The "true/false" or "right/wrong" form of question is sometimes used. Here a complete statement is given. Your job is to decide whether the statement is right or wrong.

SAMPLE: A roaming cell-phone call to a nearby city costs less than a non-roaming call to a distant city.

This statement is wrong, or false, since roaming calls are more expensive.

This is not a complete list of all possible question forms, although most of the others are variations of these common types. You will always get complete directions for answering questions. Be sure you understand *how* to mark your answers – ask questions until you do.

V. RECORDING YOUR ANSWERS

Computer terminals are used more and more today for many different kinds of exams.
For an examination with very few applicants, you may be told to record your answers in the test booklet itself. Separate answer sheets are much more common. If this separate answer sheet is to be scored by machine – and this is often the case – it is highly important that you mark your answers correctly in order to get credit.
An electronic scoring machine is often used in civil service offices because of the speed with which papers can be scored. Machine-scored answer sheets must be marked with a pencil, which will be given to you. This pencil has a high graphite content which responds to the electronic scoring machine. As a matter of fact, stray dots may register as answers, so do not let your pencil rest on the answer sheet while you are pondering the correct answer. Also, if your pencil lead breaks or is otherwise defective, ask for another.

Since the answer sheet will be dropped in a slot in the scoring machine, be careful not to bend the corners or get the paper crumpled.

The answer sheet normally has five vertical columns of numbers, with 30 numbers to a column. These numbers correspond to the question numbers in your test booklet. After each number, going across the page are four or five pairs of dotted lines. These short dotted lines have small letters or numbers above them. The first two pairs may also have a "T" or "F" above the letters. This indicates that the first two pairs only are to be used if the questions are of the true-false type. If the questions are multiple choice, disregard the "T" and "F" and pay attention only to the small letters or numbers.

Answer your questions in the manner of the sample that follows:

32. The largest city in the United States is
    A. Washington, D.C.
    B. New York City
    C. Chicago
    D. Detroit
    E. San Francisco

1) Choose the answer you think is best. (New York City is the largest, so "B" is correct.)
2) Find the row of dotted lines numbered the same as the question you are answering. (Find row number 32)
3) Find the pair of dotted lines corresponding to the answer. (Find the pair of lines under the mark "B.")
4) Make a solid black mark between the dotted lines.

VI. BEFORE THE TEST

Common sense will help you find procedures to follow to get ready for an examination. Too many of us, however, overlook these sensible measures. Indeed, nervousness and fatigue have been found to be the most serious reasons why applicants fail to do their best on civil service tests. Here is a list of reminders:

- Begin your preparation early – Don't wait until the last minute to go scurrying around for books and materials or to find out what the position is all about.
- Prepare continuously – An hour a night for a week is better than an all-night cram session. This has been definitely established. What is more, a night a week for a month will return better dividends than crowding your study into a shorter period of time.
- Locate the place of the exam – You have been sent a notice telling you when and where to report for the examination. If the location is in a different town or otherwise unfamiliar to you, it would be well to inquire the best route and learn something about the building.
- Relax the night before the test – Allow your mind to rest. Do not study at all that night. Plan some mild recreation or diversion; then go to bed early and get a good night's sleep.
- Get up early enough to make a leisurely trip to the place for the test – This way unforeseen events, traffic snarls, unfamiliar buildings, etc. will not upset you.
- Dress comfortably – A written test is not a fashion show. You will be known by number and not by name, so wear something comfortable.

- Leave excess paraphernalia at home – Shopping bags and odd bundles will get in your way. You need bring only the items mentioned in the official notice you received; usually everything you need is provided. Do not bring reference books to the exam. They will only confuse those last minutes and be taken away from you when in the test room.
- Arrive somewhat ahead of time – If because of transportation schedules you must get there very early, bring a newspaper or magazine to take your mind off yourself while waiting.
- Locate the examination room – When you have found the proper room, you will be directed to the seat or part of the room where you will sit. Sometimes you are given a sheet of instructions to read while you are waiting. Do not fill out any forms until you are told to do so; just read them and be prepared.
- Relax and prepare to listen to the instructions
- If you have any physical problem that may keep you from doing your best, be sure to tell the test administrator. If you are sick or in poor health, you really cannot do your best on the exam. You can come back and take the test some other time.

VII. AT THE TEST

The day of the test is here and you have the test booklet in your hand. The temptation to get going is very strong. Caution! There is more to success than knowing the right answers. You must know how to identify your papers and understand variations in the type of short-answer question used in this particular examination. Follow these suggestions for maximum results from your efforts:

1) Cooperate with the monitor

The test administrator has a duty to create a situation in which you can be as much at ease as possible. He will give instructions, tell you when to begin, check to see that you are marking your answer sheet correctly, and so on. He is not there to guard you, although he will see that your competitors do not take unfair advantage. He wants to help you do your best.

2) Listen to all instructions

Don't jump the gun! Wait until you understand all directions. In most civil service tests you get more time than you need to answer the questions. So don't be in a hurry. Read each word of instructions until you clearly understand the meaning. Study the examples, listen to all announcements and follow directions. Ask questions if you do not understand what to do.

3) Identify your papers

Civil service exams are usually identified by number only. You will be assigned a number; you must not put your name on your test papers. Be sure to copy your number correctly. Since more than one exam may be given, copy your exact examination title.

4) Plan your time

Unless you are told that a test is a "speed" or "rate of work" test, speed itself is usually not important. Time enough to answer all the questions will be provided, but this does not mean that you have all day. An overall time limit has been set. Divide the total time (in minutes) by the number of questions to determine the approximate time you have for each question.

5) Do not linger over difficult questions

If you come across a difficult question, mark it with a paper clip (useful to have along) and come back to it when you have been through the booklet. One caution if you do this – be sure to skip a number on your answer sheet as well. Check often to be sure that you have not lost your place and that you are marking in the row numbered the same as the question you are answering.

6) Read the questions

Be sure you know what the question asks! Many capable people are unsuccessful because they failed to *read* the questions correctly.

7) Answer all questions

Unless you have been instructed that a penalty will be deducted for incorrect answers, it is better to guess than to omit a question.

8) Speed tests

It is often better NOT to guess on speed tests. It has been found that on timed tests people are tempted to spend the last few seconds before time is called in marking answers at random – without even reading them – in the hope of picking up a few extra points. To discourage this practice, the instructions may warn you that your score will be "corrected" for guessing. That is, a penalty will be applied. The incorrect answers will be deducted from the correct ones, or some other penalty formula will be used.

9) Review your answers

If you finish before time is called, go back to the questions you guessed or omitted to give them further thought. Review other answers if you have time.

10) Return your test materials

If you are ready to leave before others have finished or time is called, take ALL your materials to the monitor and leave quietly. Never take any test material with you. The monitor can discover whose papers are not complete, and taking a test booklet may be grounds for disqualification.

VIII. EXAMINATION TECHNIQUES

1) Read the general instructions carefully. These are usually printed on the first page of the exam booklet. As a rule, these instructions refer to the timing of the examination; the fact that you should not start work until the signal and must stop work at a signal, etc. If there are any *special* instructions, such as a choice of questions to be answered, make sure that you note this instruction carefully.

2) When you are ready to start work on the examination, that is as soon as the signal has been given, read the instructions to each question booklet, underline any key words or phrases, such as *least, best, outline, describe* and the like. In this way you will tend to answer as requested rather than discover on reviewing your paper that you *listed without describing*, that you selected the *worst* choice rather than the *best* choice, etc.

3) If the examination is of the objective or multiple-choice type – that is, each question will also give a series of possible answers: A, B, C or D, and you are called upon to select the best answer and write the letter next to that answer on your answer paper – it is advisable to start answering each question in turn. There may be anywhere from 50 to 100 such questions in the three or four hours allotted and you can see how much time would be taken if you read through all the questions before beginning to answer any. Furthermore, if you come across a question or group of questions which you know would be difficult to answer, it would undoubtedly affect your handling of all the other questions.

4) If the examination is of the essay type and contains but a few questions, it is a moot point as to whether you should read all the questions before starting to answer any one. Of course, if you are given a choice – say five out of seven and the like – then it is essential to read all the questions so you can eliminate the two that are most difficult. If, however, you are asked to answer all the questions, there may be danger in trying to answer the easiest one first because you may find that you will spend too much time on it. The best technique is to answer the first question, then proceed to the second, etc.

5) Time your answers. Before the exam begins, write down the time it started, then add the time allowed for the examination and write down the time it must be completed, then divide the time available somewhat as follows:
    - If 3-1/2 hours are allowed, that would be 210 minutes. If you have 80 objective-type questions, that would be an average of 2-1/2 minutes per question. Allow yourself no more than 2 minutes per question, or a total of 160 minutes, which will permit about 50 minutes to review.
    - If for the time allotment of 210 minutes there are 7 essay questions to answer, that would average about 30 minutes a question. Give yourself only 25 minutes per question so that you have about 35 minutes to review.

6) The most important instruction is to *read each question* and make sure you know what is wanted. The second most important instruction is to *time yourself properly* so that you answer every question. The third most important instruction is to *answer every question*. Guess if you have to but include something for each question. Remember that you will receive no credit for a blank and will probably receive some credit if you write something in answer to an essay question. If you guess a letter – say "B" for a multiple-choice question – you may have guessed right. If you leave a blank as an answer to a multiple-choice question, the examiners may respect your feelings but it will not add a point to your score. Some exams may penalize you for wrong answers, so in such cases *only*, you may not want to guess unless you have some basis for your answer.

7) Suggestions
    a. Objective-type questions
        1. Examine the question booklet for proper sequence of pages and questions
        2. Read all instructions carefully
        3. Skip any question which seems too difficult; return to it after all other questions have been answered
        4. Apportion your time properly; do not spend too much time on any single question or group of questions

5. Note and underline key words – *all, most, fewest, least, best, worst, same, opposite*, etc.
6. Pay particular attention to negatives
7. Note unusual option, e.g., unduly long, short, complex, different or similar in content to the body of the question
8. Observe the use of "hedging" words – *probably, may, most likely*, etc.
9. Make sure that your answer is put next to the same number as the question
10. Do not second-guess unless you have good reason to believe the second answer is definitely more correct
11. Cross out original answer if you decide another answer is more accurate; do not erase until you are ready to hand your paper in
12. Answer all questions; guess unless instructed otherwise
13. Leave time for review

b. Essay questions
   1. Read each question carefully
   2. Determine exactly what is wanted. Underline key words or phrases.
   3. Decide on outline or paragraph answer
   4. Include many different points and elements unless asked to develop any one or two points or elements
   5. Show impartiality by giving pros and cons unless directed to select one side only
   6. Make and write down any assumptions you find necessary to answer the questions
   7. Watch your English, grammar, punctuation and choice of words
   8. Time your answers; don't crowd material

8) Answering the essay question

Most essay questions can be answered by framing the specific response around several key words or ideas. Here are a few such key words or ideas:

M's: manpower, materials, methods, money, management
P's: purpose, program, policy, plan, procedure, practice, problems, pitfalls, personnel, public relations
   a. Six basic steps in handling problems:
      1. Preliminary plan and background development
      2. Collect information, data and facts
      3. Analyze and interpret information, data and facts
      4. Analyze and develop solutions as well as make recommendations
      5. Prepare report and sell recommendations
      6. Install recommendations and follow up effectiveness

   b. Pitfalls to avoid
      1. *Taking things for granted* – A statement of the situation does not necessarily imply that each of the elements is necessarily true; for example, a complaint may be invalid and biased so that all that can be taken for granted is that a complaint has been registered

2. *Considering only one side of a situation* – Wherever possible, indicate several alternatives and then point out the reasons you selected the best one
3. *Failing to indicate follow up* – Whenever your answer indicates action on your part, make certain that you will take proper follow-up action to see how successful your recommendations, procedures or actions turn out to be
4. *Taking too long in answering any single question* – Remember to time your answers properly

IX. AFTER THE TEST

Scoring procedures differ in detail among civil service jurisdictions although the general principles are the same. Whether the papers are hand-scored or graded by machine we have described, they are nearly always graded by number. That is, the person who marks the paper knows only the number – never the name – of the applicant. Not until all the papers have been graded will they be matched with names. If other tests, such as training and experience or oral interview ratings have been given, scores will be combined. Different parts of the examination usually have different weights. For example, the written test might count 60 percent of the final grade, and a rating of training and experience 40 percent. In many jurisdictions, veterans will have a certain number of points added to their grades.

After the final grade has been determined, the names are placed in grade order and an eligible list is established. There are various methods for resolving ties between those who get the same final grade – probably the most common is to place first the name of the person whose application was received first. Job offers are made from the eligible list in the order the names appear on it. You will be notified of your grade and your rank as soon as all these computations have been made. This will be done as rapidly as possible.

People who are found to meet the requirements in the announcement are called "eligibles." Their names are put on a list of eligible candidates. An eligible's chances of getting a job depend on how high he stands on this list and how fast agencies are filling jobs from the list.

When a job is to be filled from a list of eligibles, the agency asks for the names of people on the list of eligibles for that job. When the civil service commission receives this request, it sends to the agency the names of the three people highest on this list. Or, if the job to be filled has specialized requirements, the office sends the agency the names of the top three persons who meet these requirements from the general list.

The appointing officer makes a choice from among the three people whose names were sent to him. If the selected person accepts the appointment, the names of the others are put back on the list to be considered for future openings.

That is the rule in hiring from all kinds of eligible lists, whether they are for typist, carpenter, chemist, or something else. For every vacancy, the appointing officer has his choice of any one of the top three eligibles on the list. This explains why the person whose name is on top of the list sometimes does not get an appointment when some of the persons lower on the list do. If the appointing officer chooses the second or third eligible, the No. 1 eligible does not get a job at once, but stays on the list until he is appointed or the list is terminated.

X. HOW TO PASS THE INTERVIEW TEST

The examination for which you applied requires an oral interview test. You have already taken the written test and you are now being called for the interview test – the final part of the formal examination.

You may think that it is not possible to prepare for an interview test and that there are no procedures to follow during an interview. Our purpose is to point out some things you can do in advance that will help you and some good rules to follow and pitfalls to avoid while you are being interviewed.

What is an interview supposed to test?

The written examination is designed to test the technical knowledge and competence of the candidate; the oral is designed to evaluate intangible qualities, not readily measured otherwise, and to establish a list showing the relative fitness of each candidate – as measured against his competitors – for the position sought. Scoring is not on the basis of "right" and "wrong," but on a sliding scale of values ranging from "not passable" to "outstanding." As a matter of fact, it is possible to achieve a relatively low score without a single "incorrect" answer because of evident weakness in the qualities being measured.

Occasionally, an examination may consist entirely of an oral test – either an individual or a group oral. In such cases, information is sought concerning the technical knowledges and abilities of the candidate, since there has been no written examination for this purpose. More commonly, however, an oral test is used to supplement a written examination.

Who conducts interviews?

The composition of oral boards varies among different jurisdictions. In nearly all, a representative of the personnel department serves as chairman. One of the members of the board may be a representative of the department in which the candidate would work. In some cases, "outside experts" are used, and, frequently, a businessman or some other representative of the general public is asked to serve. Labor and management or other special groups may be represented. The aim is to secure the services of experts in the appropriate field.

However the board is composed, it is a good idea (and not at all improper or unethical) to ascertain in advance of the interview who the members are and what groups they represent. When you are introduced to them, you will have some idea of their backgrounds and interests, and at least you will not stutter and stammer over their names.

What should be done before the interview?

While knowledge about the board members is useful and takes some of the surprise element out of the interview, there is other preparation which is more substantive. It *is* possible to prepare for an oral interview – in several ways:

1) Keep a copy of your application and review it carefully before the interview

This may be the only document before the oral board, and the starting point of the interview. Know what education and experience you have listed there, and the sequence and dates of all of it. Sometimes the board will ask you to review the highlights of your experience for them; you should not have to hem and haw doing it.

2) Study the class specification and the examination announcement

Usually, the oral board has one or both of these to guide them. The qualities, characteristics or knowledges required by the position sought are stated in these documents. They offer valuable clues as to the nature of the oral interview. For example, if the job involves supervisory responsibilities, the announcement will usually indicate that knowledge of modern supervisory methods and the qualifications of the candidate as a supervisor will be tested. If so, you can expect such questions, frequently in the form of a hypothetical situation which you are expected to solve. NEVER go into an oral without knowledge of the duties and responsibilities of the job you seek.

3) Think through each qualification required
Try to visualize the kind of questions you would ask if you were a board member. How well could you answer them? Try especially to appraise your own knowledge and background in each area, *measured against the job sought*, and identify any areas in which you are weak. Be critical and realistic – do not flatter yourself.

4) Do some general reading in areas in which you feel you may be weak
For example, if the job involves supervision and your past experience has NOT, some general reading in supervisory methods and practices, particularly in the field of human relations, might be useful. Do NOT study agency procedures or detailed manuals. The oral board will be testing your understanding and capacity, not your memory.

5) Get a good night's sleep and watch your general health and mental attitude
You will want a clear head at the interview. Take care of a cold or any other minor ailment, and of course, no hangovers.

What should be done on the day of the interview?
Now comes the day of the interview itself. Give yourself plenty of time to get there. Plan to arrive somewhat ahead of the scheduled time, particularly if your appointment is in the fore part of the day. If a previous candidate fails to appear, the board might be ready for you a bit early. By early afternoon an oral board is almost invariably behind schedule if there are many candidates, and you may have to wait. Take along a book or magazine to read, or your application to review, but leave any extraneous material in the waiting room when you go in for your interview. In any event, relax and compose yourself.

The matter of dress is important. The board is forming impressions about you – from your experience, your manners, your attitude, and your appearance. Give your personal appearance careful attention. Dress your best, but not your flashiest. Choose conservative, appropriate clothing, and be sure it is immaculate. This is a business interview, and your appearance should indicate that you regard it as such. Besides, being well groomed and properly dressed will help boost your confidence.

Sooner or later, someone will call your name and escort you into the interview room. *This is it.* From here on you are on your own. It is too late for any more preparation. But remember, you asked for this opportunity to prove your fitness, and you are here because your request was granted.

What happens when you go in?
The usual sequence of events will be as follows: The clerk (who is often the board stenographer) will introduce you to the chairman of the oral board, who will introduce you to the other members of the board. Acknowledge the introductions before you sit down. Do not be surprised if you find a microphone facing you or a stenotypist sitting by. Oral interviews are usually recorded in the event of an appeal or other review.

Usually the chairman of the board will open the interview by reviewing the highlights of your education and work experience from your application – primarily for the benefit of the other members of the board, as well as to get the material into the record. Do not interrupt or comment unless there is an error or significant misinterpretation; if that is the case, do not hesitate. But do not quibble about insignificant matters. Also, he will usually ask you some question about your education, experience or your present job – partly to get you to start talking and to establish the interviewing "rapport." He may start the actual questioning, or turn it over to one of the other members. Frequently, each member undertakes the questioning on a particular area, one in which he is perhaps most competent, so you can expect each member to participate in the examination. Because time is limited, you may also expect some rather abrupt switches in the direction the questioning takes, so do not be upset by it. Normally, a board member will not pursue a single line of questioning unless he discovers a particular strength or weakness.

After each member has participated, the chairman will usually ask whether any member has any further questions, then will ask you if you have anything you wish to add. Unless you are expecting this question, it may floor you. Worse, it may start you off on an extended, extemporaneous speech. The board is not usually seeking more information. The question is principally to offer you a last opportunity to present further qualifications or to indicate that you have nothing to add. So, if you feel that a significant qualification or characteristic has been overlooked, it is proper to point it out in a sentence or so. Do not compliment the board on the thoroughness of their examination – they have been sketchy, and you know it. If you wish, merely say, "No thank you, I have nothing further to add." This is a point where you can "talk yourself out" of a good impression or fail to present an important bit of information. Remember, *you close the interview yourself*.

The chairman will then say, "That is all, Mr. _____, thank you." Do not be startled; the interview is over, and quicker than you think. Thank him, gather your belongings and take your leave. Save your sigh of relief for the other side of the door.

How to put your best foot forward
Throughout this entire process, you may feel that the board individually and collectively is trying to pierce your defenses, seek out your hidden weaknesses and embarrass and confuse you. Actually, this is not true. They are obliged to make an appraisal of your qualifications for the job you are seeking, and they want to see you in your best light. Remember, they must interview all candidates and a non-cooperative candidate may become a failure in spite of their best efforts to bring out his qualifications. Here are 15 suggestions that will help you:

1) Be natural – Keep your attitude confident, not cocky
If you are not confident that you can do the job, do not expect the board to be. Do not apologize for your weaknesses, try to bring out your strong points. The board is interested in a positive, not negative, presentation. Cockiness will antagonize any board member and make him wonder if you are covering up a weakness by a false show of strength.

2) Get comfortable, but don't lounge or sprawl
Sit erectly but not stiffly. A careless posture may lead the board to conclude that you are careless in other things, or at least that you are not impressed by the importance of the occasion. Either conclusion is natural, even if incorrect. Do not fuss with your clothing, a pencil or an ashtray. Your hands may occasionally be useful to emphasize a point; do not let them become a point of distraction.

3) Do not wisecrack or make small talk
This is a serious situation, and your attitude should show that you consider it as such. Further, the time of the board is limited – they do not want to waste it, and neither should you.

4) Do not exaggerate your experience or abilities

In the first place, from information in the application or other interviews and sources, the board may know more about you than you think. Secondly, you probably will not get away with it. An experienced board is rather adept at spotting such a situation, so do not take the chance.

5) If you know a board member, do not make a point of it, yet do not hide it

Certainly you are not fooling him, and probably not the other members of the board. Do not try to take advantage of your acquaintanceship – it will probably do you little good.

6) Do not dominate the interview

Let the board do that. They will give you the clues – do not assume that you have to do all the talking. Realize that the board has a number of questions to ask you, and do not try to take up all the interview time by showing off your extensive knowledge of the answer to the first one.

7) Be attentive

You only have 20 minutes or so, and you should keep your attention at its sharpest throughout. When a member is addressing a problem or question to you, give him your undivided attention. Address your reply principally to him, but do not exclude the other board members.

8) Do not interrupt

A board member may be stating a problem for you to analyze. He will ask you a question when the time comes. Let him state the problem, and wait for the question.

9) Make sure you understand the question

Do not try to answer until you are sure what the question is. If it is not clear, restate it in your own words or ask the board member to clarify it for you. However, do not haggle about minor elements.

10) Reply promptly but not hastily

A common entry on oral board rating sheets is "candidate responded readily," or "candidate hesitated in replies." Respond as promptly and quickly as you can, but do not jump to a hasty, ill-considered answer.

11) Do not be peremptory in your answers

A brief answer is proper – but do not fire your answer back. That is a losing game from your point of view. The board member can probably ask questions much faster than you can answer them.

12) Do not try to create the answer you think the board member wants

He is interested in what kind of mind you have and how it works – not in playing games. Furthermore, he can usually spot this practice and will actually grade you down on it.

13) Do not switch sides in your reply merely to agree with a board member

Frequently, a member will take a contrary position merely to draw you out and to see if you are willing and able to defend your point of view. Do not start a debate, yet do not surrender a good position. If a position is worth taking, it is worth defending.

14) Do not be afraid to admit an error in judgment if you are shown to be wrong

The board knows that you are forced to reply without any opportunity for careful consideration. Your answer may be demonstrably wrong. If so, admit it and get on with the interview.

15) Do not dwell at length on your present job

The opening question may relate to your present assignment. Answer the question but do not go into an extended discussion. You are being examined for a *new* job, not your present one. As a matter of fact, try to phrase ALL your answers in terms of the job for which you are being examined.

Basis of Rating

Probably you will forget most of these "do's" and "don'ts" when you walk into the oral interview room. Even remembering them all will not ensure you a passing grade. Perhaps you did not have the qualifications in the first place. But remembering them will help you to put your best foot forward, without treading on the toes of the board members.

Rumor and popular opinion to the contrary notwithstanding, an oral board wants you to make the best appearance possible. They know you are under pressure – but they also want to see how you respond to it as a guide to what your reaction would be under the pressures of the job you seek. They will be influenced by the degree of poise you display, the personal traits you show and the manner in which you respond.

ABOUT THIS BOOK

This book contains tests divided into Examination Sections. Go through each test, answering every question in the margin. We have also attached a sample answer sheet at the back of the book that can be removed and used. At the end of each test look at the answer key and check your answers. On the ones you got wrong, look at the right answer choice and learn. Do not fill in the answers first. Do not memorize the questions and answers, but understand the answer and principles involved. On your test, the questions will likely be different from the samples. Questions are changed and new ones added. If you understand these past questions you should have success with any changes that arise. Tests may consist of several types of questions. We have additional books on each subject should more study be advisable or necessary for you. Finally, the more you study, the better prepared you will be. This book is intended to be the last thing you study before you walk into the examination room. Prior study of relevant texts is also recommended. NLC publishes some of these in our Fundamental Series. Knowledge and good sense are important factors in passing your exam. Good luck also helps. So now study this Passbook, absorb the material contained within and take that knowledge into the examination. Then do your best to pass that exam.

EXAMINATION SECTION

EXAMINATION SECTION
TEST 1

DIRECTIONS: Each question or incomplete statement is followed by several suggested answers of completions. Select the one that BEST answers the question or complete the statement. PRINT THE LETTER OF THE CORRECT ANSWER IN THE SPACE AT THE RIGHT.

1. Three point perspective drawing has _____ converging point(s).　　　　1._____
   A. 1
   B. 2
   C. 3
   D. 4

2. In structural drafting, section lines are used to represent　　　　2._____
   A. cross sectional cuts
   B. hidden features
   C. hidden planes
   D. cross sectional theoretical cuts

3. Which of the following is purely a draft file format?　　　　3._____
   A. .dwg
   B. .igs
   C. .iges
   D. .stl

4. In third angle projections, the plane of projection is　　　　4._____
   A. no projection plane
   B. in between the observer and object
   C. below the object
   D. before the observer

5. Architectural "A" size sheet has the dimensions of　　　　5._____
   A. Size = 8 x 11
   B. Size = 8-1/2 x 11-1/2
   C. Size = 8-1/2 x 11
   D. Size = 8 x 11

6. Bilateral means two _____.　　　　6._____
   A. edges
   B. sides
   C. corners
   D. radii

7. Symbol of "BOM" on a draft means　　　　7._____
   A. base of material
   B. bills of manufacturing
   C. budget of manufacturing
   D. bill of material

1

8. Changing from 2D to 3D in CAD means
    A. changing drawing standards
    B. giving height to planer sketch
    C. changing lengths
    D. changing software settings

9. DIN is a _____ CAD standard.
    A. British
    B. SI
    C. German
    D. Japanese

10. Workplanes in CAD software are the same as
    A. cross sections
    B. sketches
    C. drafting layers
    D. floors

11. In CAD software, trim command is part of a _____ panel.
    A. sketch
    B. draw
    C. modify
    D. it is available in all panels

12. Tapering function in CAD requires
    A. draft plane
    B. draft direction
    C. either draft plane or draft direction
    D. both draft plane and draft direction

13. Copilot snapping refers to a change in which of the following?
    A. Line color and thickness
    B. Cursor color and shape
    C. Screen color and shape
    D. Layer color and thickness

14. CADD software offers at least _____ different views of the drawing.
    A. 6
    B. 5
    C. 7
    D. 8

15. A CAM module generates the
    A. production instructions
    B. machine code
    C. manufacturing instructions
    D. G codes and M codes

16. What is the "Layer Cake Approach" in CAD? 16._____
    A. Building the part on entirely separate layers
    B. Removing the part layer by layer
    C. Splitting a part into layers
    D. Building the part by adding feature on previous layers

17. What is the basic difference between sweep and loft? 17._____
    A. Sweep is complex; loft is simple
    B. Loft is a user-dragable tool
    C. Loft can have multiple profiles
    D. Sweep can have multiple paths

18. What are the benefits of using CAD tools over traditional drawing methods? 18._____
    A. They are more efficient for the drafter
    B. Computer tools allow more proficiency and freedom
    C. They offer standardized formats
    D. All of the above

19. Pull command would be the same as 19._____
    A. revolve
    B. remove
    C. sweep
    D. extrude

20. Which one of the following is not an input parameter for radial patterns? 20._____
    A. Axis
    B. Offset
    C. Rectangular increment
    D. Shape of pattern

21. Trimetric view shows the object such that 21._____
    A. all the sides are equal
    B. all the sides are not equal
    C. all the angles are equal
    D. it provides the planer view of the object

22. Which one is preferred from a manufacturing point of view? 22._____
    A. Blend over chamfer
    B. Chamfer over blend
    C. Taper over chamfer
    D. Chamfer over blend and taper

23. Which of these is a one point command? 23._____
    A. Line
    B. Circle
    C. Arc
    D. Construction line

24. Which of the following cannot be adjusted in Initial System Settings?
    A. Drawing zones
    B. Drafting standards
    C. Draft formats
    D. All of the above

25. Self-intersecting surfaces are monitored by
    A. check manufacturing operations tool
    B. check parts tool
    C. check dimensions tool
    D. CAD software does not check this.

KEY (CORRECT ANSWERS)

1.	C	11.	C
2.	D	12.	C
3.	A	13.	B
4.	B	14.	C
5.	C	15.	D
6.	B	16.	D
7.	D	17.	C
8.	B	18.	D
9.	C	19.	D
10.	C	20.	C

21.	B
22.	B
23.	B
24.	C
25.	B

TEST 2

DIRECTIONS: Each question or incomplete statement is followed by several suggested answers of completions. Select the one that BEST answers the question or complete the statement. PRINT THE LETTER OF THE CORRECT ANSWER IN THE SPACE AT THE RIGHT.

1. Section lines can also be referred as _____ lines. 1._____
    A. hidden
    B. phantom
    C. cross section
    D. cutting

2. Architectural "B" size sheet has the dimensions of 2._____
    A. Size = 11 x 15
    B. Size = 11 x 17
    C. Size = 17 x 11
    D. Size = 17 x 15

3. _____ lines are not part of the main draft. 3._____
    A. Hidden
    B. Section
    C. Construction
    D. Reference

4. Universal format for CAD is 4._____
    A. .txt
    B. .iges
    C. .stl
    D. .dwg

5. Units, number of layers and layer styles are basically required for drawing _____. 5._____
    A. standards
    B. layouts
    C. settings
    D. format

6. Chamfer feature in CAD can be defined by 6._____
    A. angle to face
    B. edge length
    C. either of the above
    D. both of the above

7. What is the horizontal surface angle for isometrics drawings? 7._____
    A. 30 degrees
    B. 45 degrees
    C. 60 degrees
    D. No fixed standard

8. _____ is the basic tool in CAD software to change a sketch in a model.
   A. Extrude
   B. Chamfer
   C. Blend
   D. Shell

9. Which of the following is the commonly followed design standard in the US?
   A. ANSI
   B. JIS
   C. DIN
   D. SI

10. What information is not conveyed by snap function?
    A. Bi section
    B. Layer
    C. End point
    D. Corner lines

11. Spline is a _____ function.
    A. linear
    B. mathematical
    C. interpolation
    D. algebraic

12. Blind hole in CAD parts is a hole
    A. drawn as a hidden feature
    B. that is not visible in front view
    C. that is not visible in top view
    D. that does not go through all of the material

13. CAD Designer can have minimum _____ different views of the drawing.
    A. 6
    B. 5
    C. 7
    D. 8

14. What is the potter's wheel approach in CAD?
    A. Revolving a 2D to make a desired model
    B. Removing material to make a desired model
    C. Using Boolean operators to make a desired model
    D. Adding material to make a desired model

15. Sweep cross section should be
    A. symmetrical
    B. normal to the path
    C. closed
    D. smaller than the path size

16. Loft is an extended form of
    A. revolve
    B. sweep
    C. taper
    D. pull

    16._____

17. What is the difference between punch command and stamp command?
    A. Punch removes material outside the profile
    B. Punch is 3D and stamp is 2D
    C. Stamp removes material outside the profile
    D. There is no difference

    17._____

18. Pull angular command would be the same as
    A. extrude angular
    B. revolve
    C. sweep
    D. helix

    18._____

19. Orthographic projection always has the same dimensions as of the dimensions of object because projection lines are
    A. parallel to plane
    B. parallel to observer
    C. perpendicular with each other
    D. perpendicular to plane

    19._____

20. Which file type is used to transfer a CAD file for CAM?
    A. .dwg
    B. .stl
    C. .env
    D. .pk

    20._____

21. What is the difference between counter-bore and counter-sink?
    A. Counter-bore increases the hole diameter conically; counter-sink increases the hole diameter cylindrically
    B. Counter-bore increases the hole diameter cylindrically; counter-sink increases the hole diameter conically
    C. Counter-bore decreases the hole diameter conically; counter-sink decreases the hole diameter cylindrically
    D. Counter-bore decreases the hole diameter conically; counter-sink increases the hole diameter conically

    21._____

22. Which of the following statements is NOT true for 3D wireframes?
    A. It is an extension of 2D drafting
    B. It is an extension of 3D modeling
    C. It has no mass properties
    D. Features cannot be directly added in it

    22._____

23. What is the function of the mate tool?
    A. Joining parts together
    B. Aligning surfaces together
    C. Position surfaces as desired
    D. All of the above

24. Trim can also be used as
    A. delete
    B. remove
    C. boolean subtract
    D. all of the above

25. Layer cake approach requires expertise in
    A. drafting
    B. modeling
    C. manufacturing
    D. assembling

KEY (CORRECT ANSWERS)

1.	B	11.	B
2.	B	12.	D
3.	C	13.	C
4.	B	14.	A
5.	C	15.	C
6.	C	16.	B
7.	A	17.	C
8.	A	18.	B
9.	A	19.	D
10.	B	20.	B

21.	B
22.	B
23.	A
24.	A
25.	B

TEST 3

DIRECTIONS: Each question or incomplete statement is followed by several suggested answers of completions. Select the one that BEST answers the question or complete the statement. PRINT THE LETTER OF THE CORRECT ANSWER IN THE SPACE AT THE RIGHT.

1. Object lines are also called _____ lines.
    A. feature
    B. visible
    C. contour
    D. fix

    1._____

2. Line weight is maximum for _____ lines.
    A. centre
    B. construction
    C. hidden
    D. object

    2._____

3. "TOL" symbol on an architectural draft represents
    A. tool specification
    B. tolerance
    C. tools list
    D. test organizations list

    3._____

4. Architectural "C" size sheet has the dimensions of
    A. Size = 22 x 34
    B. Size = 17 x 22
    C. Size = 8-1/2 x 11
    D. Size = 11 x 17

    4._____

5. Observer – Plane – Object is the orientation for _____ projections.
    A. first angle
    B. isometric
    C. third angle
    D. perspective

    5._____

6. Area, number of views and orientation of views are features that define drawing
    A. standards
    B. layouts
    C. settings
    D. format

    6._____

7. To draw a fillet on draft, you need to define its   7._____
   A. curvature
   B. interior radius
   C. side length
   D. exterior radius

8. What is the main difference between a "sketch" and "model" in CAD?   8._____
   A. Different standards
   B. Increased number of dimensions
   C. Increased measurements
   D. Change in the perspective of observer

9. CAD offers _____ planer views of the object.   9._____
   A. 3
   B. 4
   C. 5
   D. 6

10. What is the basic CAD tool for the "Potter's wheel" approach?   10._____
    A. Extrude
    B. Remove
    C. Sweep
    D. Revolve

11. What is the basic CAD tool for "Layer Cake" approach?   11._____
    A. Extrude
    B. Remove
    C. Sweep
    D. Revolve

12. What are the input parameters for counter-bore?   12._____
    A. Diameter and depth
    B. Diameter and angle
    C. Diameter increment and tangent direction
    D. Diameter reduction and angle

13. Orthographic projection has projection lines that are   13._____
    A. parallel to plane
    B. parallel to observer
    C. perpendicular with each other
    D. perpendicular to plane

14. Dimetric view shows the object such that
    A. any two angles are equal
    B. any two angles are equal
    C. any two sides and angles are equal
    D. any two sides and angles are unequal

    14._____

15. View port does not contain
    A. features info
    B. history
    C. layers
    D. annotations

    15._____

16. Which two features are the same from a manufacturing point of view?
    A. Chamfer and blend
    B. Blend and fillet
    C. Revolve and sweep
    D. Sweep and loft

    16._____

17. Which statement is NOT true about CAD Boolean functions?
    A. They unite two parts
    B. They subtract two parts
    C. They find the intersecting region
    D. They can assemble the parts

    17._____

18. Shell command in CAD
    A. increases the number dimensions of part
    B. increases the number of faces in part
    C. adds material to the part
    D. decreases the dimensions of part

    18._____

19. Sweep command works by
    A. extrapolating the cross section on defined path
    B. extending the cross section on defined path
    C. extruding the cross section on defined path
    D. revolving the cross section on defined path

    19._____

20. Dynamic positioning tools allow the user to work on _____ degrees of freedom.
    A. 3
    B. 4
    C. 5
    D. 6

    20._____

21. What is not an input parameter for Helix tool?
    A. Axis
    B. Path
    C. Turns
    D. Pitch

    21._____

22. Trim command is available in
    A. Sketch panel
    B. Draw panel
    C. Modify panel
    D. Model pane

    22._____

23. Which statement is not true about the loft command? 23._____
    A. Loft can have multiple cross sections
    B. Loft is an extension of sweep command
    C. Loft only work on single path
    D. Loft can have multiple profiles

24. CAD tools make 3D models by 24._____
    A. mathematical parameters
    B. geometrical features
    C. structural parameters
    D. manufacturing parameters

25. Which method is preferred from a "usage" point of view? 25._____
    A. Blend over chamfer
    B. Chamfer over blend
    C. Taper over chamfer
    D. Chamfer over blend and taper

KEY (CORRECT ANSWERS)

1.	B		11.	A
2.	D		12.	A
3.	B		13.	D
4.	B		14.	C
5.	C		15.	B
6.	B		16.	B
7.	B		17.	D
8.	B		18.	B
9.	D		19.	C
10.	D		20.	D

21.	B
22.	C
23.	C
24.	B
25.	A

TEST 4

DIRECTIONS: Each question or incomplete statement is followed by several suggested answers of completions. Select the one that BEST answers the question or complete the statement. PRINT THE LETTER OF THE CORRECT ANSWER IN THE SPACE AT THE RIGHT.

1. The term "Poche" is used for _____ in architectural drafts. 1._____
    A. borders
    B. material information
    C. textural patterns
    D. size information

2. To draw an architectural floor plan, which feature of CAD software is used? 2._____
    A. Annotation
    B. Layer
    C. Sketch
    D. Model

3. Architectural "D" size sheet has the dimensions of 3._____
    A. Size = 21 x 34
    B. Size = 20 x 34
    C. Size = 22 x 30
    D. Size = 22 x 34

4. Observer – Object – Plane is an example of _____ projections. 4._____
    A. first angle
    B. isometric
    C. third angle
    D. perspective

5. CAD tools are NOT used for 5._____
    A. simulations
    B. analysis
    C. HR Estimation
    D. visualization

6. ANSI stands for 6._____
    A. American National Standards Implementation
    B. American Northern Standards Institute
    C. American National Standards Institute
    D. American Nationals Standardization and Implementation

7. Which of the following software is NOT used for drafting purposes?   7._____
   A. Inventor   C. Visual Studio
   B. Solid Edge   D. Pro-E

8. Computerized systems represent different layers of a draft by different   8._____
   A. symbols   C. levels
   B. names   D. colors

9. How many degrees of freedom a CAD tool can offer to any object?   9._____
   A. 3   C. 5
   B. 4   D. 6

10. Sweep is an extended form of   10._____
    A. extrude
    B. revolve
    C. helix
    D. loft

11. Designers can use both layer cake and potter's wheel approach while making   11._____
    parts in CAD. The preferred approach will depend on
    A. complexity of the design
    B. CAD tools
    C. product requirements
    D. all of the above

12. Potter's wheel approach requires expertise in   12._____
    A. drafting
    B. modeling
    C. manufacturing
    D. assembling

13. Which of the following is true for 3D wireframes?   13._____
    A. It is an extension of 2D drafting
    B. It is an extension of 3D modeling
    C. It has same mass properties as 3D model
    D. Features can be directly added in it

14. What are the input parameters for counter-sink feature?   14._____
    A. Diameter and depth
    B. Diameter and angle
    C. Diameter increment and tangent direction
    D. Diameter reduction and angle

15. Which of the following statements is NOT true regarding punch command?   15._____
    A. Punch removes material inside the profile
    B. Punch is an extension of extrude command
    C. Stamp removes material outside the profile
    D. Punch and stamp are same

16. A slot can be defined by   16._____
    A. one center point and vertical offset
    B. two center points and vertical offset
    C. two center points and horizontal offset
    D. one center point and horizontal offset

17. Which two features are the same from a manufacturing point of view?   17._____
    A. Chamfer and blend
    B. Drill and bore
    C. Revolve and sweep
    D. Sweep and loft

18. Boolean functions allow the user to   18._____
    A. unite two parts
    B. subtract two parts
    C. find the intersecting region
    D. all of the above

19. CAD software checks for self-intersecting surfaces by   19._____
    A. check dimensions tool
    B. CAD software does not check this
    C. check manufacturing operations tool
    D. check parts tool

20. "Parent-Child" term in CAD is used for   20._____
    A. actual feature and derived feature
    B. actual part and derived part
    C. actual draft and derived draft
    D. all of the above

21. GA is the symbol for: 21._____
    A. Gain
    B. Gauge
    C. General Alignment
    D. General Annotations

22. IGES stands for:
    A. Initial Graphics Exchange Standard
    B. Initial Graphics Exchange Specification
    C. International Graphics Exchange Standards
    D. Initial Graphics Estimation Specifications

    22._____

23. Mating feature in assembly tools can
    A. join parts together
    B. align surfaces together
    C. position surfaces as desired
    D. perform all of the above functions

    23._____

24. Line weight is minimum for _____ lines.
    A. centre
    B. construction
    C. section
    D. object

    24._____

25. For shell command in CAD, offset is
    A. uniform for all sides
    B. larger for top side
    C. larger for bottom side
    D. larger for bottom side and same for side walls

    25._____

KEY (CORRECT ANSWERS)

1.	C		11.	A
2.	B		12.	A
3.	D		13.	A
4.	A		14.	B
5.	C		15.	D
6.	C		16.	C
7.	C		17.	B
8.	D		18.	D
9.	D		19.	D
10.	B		20.	D

21.	B
22.	B
23.	B
24.	B
25.	A

EXAMINATION SECTION
TEST 1

DIRECTIONS: Each question or incomplete statement is followed by several suggested answers of completions. Select the one that BEST answers the question or complete the statement. PRINT THE LETTER OF THE CORRECT ANSWER IN THE SPACE AT THE RIGHT.

1. Geographic information is
    A. linear
    B. one-dimensional
    C. multi-dimensional
    D. none of the above

    1._____

2. GIS is an abbreviation of
    A. Global Integration System
    B. Global Information System
    C. Geographic Information Standards
    D. Geographic Information System

    2._____

3. Two main data types in GIS are
    A. images and graphics
    B. vector and maps
    C. vector and raster
    D. latitude and longitude

    3._____

4. Vector data consists of:
    A. land maps and images
    B. satellite images
    C. postal codes, latitude and longitude
    D. points, lines and polygons

    4._____

5. Three stages of executing GIS are
    A. taking, uploading and viewing images
    B. latitudes, longitudes and postal codes
    C. data preparation, analysis and presentation
    D. data, information and knowledge

    5._____

6. GPS is an abbreviation of
    A. Geographic Positioning System
    B. Global Positioning Standard
    C. Geographic Planning System
    D. Global Positioning System

    6._____

7. A map is a
    A. database of locations
    B. set of geographic images
    C. miniature representation of some part of the real world
    D. grid of values

    7._____

17

8. The database used for GIS is called
   A. Spatial Database
   B. General Database
   C. Map Database
   D. Positioning Database

9. GIS is a system capable of
   A. storing and displaying an individual's bio-data
   B. storing, displaying and manipulating data related to space
   C. assembling, storing, manipulating and displaying geographically referenced information
   D. assembling, storing, manipulating and displaying environmentally referenced data

10. Decreasing the map scale would
    A. show more detail
    B. show less detail
    C. would not have any effect
    D. none of the above

11. Data is geo-referenced when it is
    A. tagged
    B. analyzed
    C. associated with a position using spatial reference system
    D. retrieved

12. Geo-coding is the process of
    A. writing any program for GIS
    B. finding associated geographic coordinates of data
    C. encrypting location data
    D. viewing data on maps

13. Raster data consists of
    A. location information
    B. data tables
    C. a sorted grid of different values making up an image
    D. vegetation and land maps

14. Which of the following is NOT a component of a geodatabase?
    A. Relationship classes
    B. Shapefile
    C. Geographic features
    D. Attribute data

15. COGO data entry refers to
    A. entering data by using coordinate geometery
    B. entering data by using coordinal geography
    C. software for data entry
    D. none of the above

16. The relationship between the directions on the map and the corresponding compass directions is called
    A. map scale
    B. orientation of a map
    C. GPS
    D. COGO

17. The process of converting geographic features on an analog map into digital format is known as map _____.
    A. orientation
    B. organization
    C. digitization
    D. conversion

18. The data format DRG is an acronym of
    A. Digital Reclassification Graphics
    B. Digital Record Graphics
    C. Digital Raster Graphics
    D. Documented Record Graphics

19. DOQ is used in GIS when a map shows
    A. topographic map
    B. base map
    C. aerial photography
    D. polygons

20. Which of the following is NOT a type of attribute data?
    A. BLOB
    B. Date
    C. Integer
    D. OLE

21. _____ is known as the father of GIS.
    A. John Snow
    B. Howard T. Fisher
    C. ESRI
    D. Dr. Roger Tomlinson

22. GeoRSS refers to
    A. geographic images
    B. raster data file
    C. standard for encoding location as part of a web feed
    D. standard for decoding the location into non-spatial formats

23. XML notation for expressing geographic annotation is called
    A. GML
    B. KML
    C. Shape file
    D. XGML

24. TIGER file format is an example of
    A. raster data
    B. topographic map
    C. vector data
    D. non-spatial data

25. A set of reference points on the Earth's surface against which position measurements are made is known as
    A. COGO
    B. geodetic datum
    C. map base
    D. map reference

KEY (CORRECT ANSWERS)

1. C
2. D
3. C
4. D
5. C

6. D
7. C
8. A
9. C
10. B

11. C
12. B
13. C
14. A
15. A

16. B
17. C
18. C
19. C
20. D

21. D
22. C
23. B
24. C
25. B

TEST 2

DIRECTIONS: Each question or incomplete statement is followed by several suggested answers of completions. Select the one that BEST answers the question or complete the statement. PRINT THE LETTER OF THE CORRECT ANSWER IN THE SPACE AT THE RIGHT.

1. Which one of the following is NOT an example of spatial data? 1._____
    A. Lines and Polygons
    B. Points showing locations
    C. Satellite images
    D. Times of specific events

2. Cartography is defined as 2._____
    A. storing location data
    B. an art of drawing maps
    C. storing data in a cart
    D. retrieving location data

3. Acquisition of information without making physical contact is known as 3._____
    A. GIS
    B. remote sensing
    C. virtual information
    D. GPS

4. Pixel size is measure of 4._____
    A. map distance
    B. polygons
    C. spatial resolution
    D. GPS

5. Aligning geographic data to a known coordinate system is called 5._____
    A. geo-coding
    B. geo-caching
    C. GPS
    D. geo-referencing

6. Web environments allowing access to geo-spatial information are called 6._____
    A. GIS servers
    B. web-GIS clients
    C. spatial databases
    D. none of the above

7. A photograph of earth's surface taken from an object flying above is called a(n) 7._____
    A. geo-photograph
    B. aerial photograph
    C. still photograph
    D. GIS image

21

8. Process of converting raster data into vector data is known as
   A. rasterization
   B. vectorization
   C. geo-conversion
   D. none of the above

8._____

9. Two types of geographic data fields are
   A. vector and raster
   B. long and short
   C. discrete and continuous
   D. latitude and longitude

9._____

10. A base map is
    A. a map of a base camp
    B. a basic map
    C. any map containing geographic features for geographical reference
    D. none of the above

10._____

11. Secondary sources of GIS data are
    A. sources collected in digital format
    B. digital and analog datasets originally captured for another purpose and have to be converted in proper format
    C. datasets collected from web as shape file
    D. GIS datasets that are captured without human physical contact

11._____

12. A survey that provides information about relative locations and features of land is called a _____ survey.
    A. land
    B. topographic
    C. population
    D. geo-

12._____

13. Geo-coding service is used for
    A. converting spatial data into descriptive addresses
    B. converting non-spatial descriptions of places into spatial data
    C. conversion of analog map into digital
    D. coding for GIS

13._____

14. The process of adding geographical metadata to different media is known as geo-_____.
    A. tagging
    B. coding
    C. fencing
    D. tracking

14._____

15. An attribute table consists of
    A. address codes
    B. personality attributes
    C. values representing geographic features
    D. values showing map projections

15._____

16. Which of the following has a single attribute assigned to each cell in the raster that defines which c category the cell belongs to?
    A. Continuous raster data
    B. Discrete raster data
    C. Integer raster data
    D. Continuous vector data

17. ArcGIS refers to
    A. a standard protocol for serving geo-referenced map images over the Internet
    B. a platform for designing and managing solutions through application of geographic knowledge
    C. satellite imagery for geographic analysis
    D. GPS simulation tool

18. OpenStreetMap is an example of _____ web maps.
    A. personalized
    B. distributed
    C. collaborative
    D. user

19. A standard protocol for serving geo-referenced map images over the Internet is
    A. ArcGIS
    B. Web Map Service
    C. Web Map Client
    D. Map protocol

20. Coordinate transformation between two vector spaces in GIS is done through
    A. angle transformation
    B. affine transformation
    C. image transformation
    D. position transformation

21. Information needed for a GPS receiver to calculate the position downloaded from satellite every day is called _____ data.
    A. almanac
    B. affine
    C. ephemeris
    D. raster

22. Nearest Neighbor method is an example of
    A. geo-statistical interpolation
    B. non-geostatistical interpolation
    C. geographic interpolator
    D. univariate interpolator

23. In GPS, a file transmitted from a satellite to a receiver that contains information about precise orbits of all satellites is known as _____ data.
    A. vector
    B. almanac
    C. ephemeris
    D. affinity

24. The method to determine the origins of the value of a continuous attribute is   24._____
    A. interpolation
    B. Nearest Neighbor
    C. Factorial Kriging
    D. Block Kriging

25. The geo-database of ArcGIS uses _____ database.   25._____
    A. relational
    B. object relational
    C. simple
    D. multi-dimensional

KEY (CORRECT ANSWERS)

1.	D	11.	B
2.	B	12.	B
3.	B	13.	B
4.	C	14.	A
5.	D	15.	C
6.	B	16.	B
7.	B	17.	B
8.	B	18.	C
9.	C	19.	B
10.	C	20.	B

21. A
22. A
23. C
24. C
25. B

TEST 3

DIRECTIONS: Each question or incomplete statement is followed by several suggested answers of completions. Select the one that BEST answers the question or complete the statement. PRINT THE LETTER OF THE CORRECT ANSWER IN THE SPACE AT THE RIGHT.

1. Google Places API is used for
   A. searching points of interest
   B. geocoding
   C. tracking path
   D. finding directions

   1._____

2. Location analytics refers to
   A. analyzing location statistics
   B. analyzing population with reference to geography
   C. analyzing data of land
   D. adding a geographic dimension to business analytics

   2._____

3. Which of the following geographic information would NOT be found by involving GIS?
   A. Knowing criminal activities in a particular area
   B. Knowing how much land area in Pakistan has been urbanized
   C. Estimating the population of Pakistan in 2015
   D. Determining the number of health facilities in a particular area

   3._____

4. Two basic types of map information in GIS are
   A. spatial and non-spatial
   B. geographic and personal
   C. spatial and personal
   D. attribute and non-attribute

   4._____

5. The art of surveying the earth's surface considering its shape and size is known as
   A. Earth survey
   B. geographic survey
   C. geodetic survey
   D. geomapping

   5._____

6. In cartography, any network of parallel and perpendicular lines superimposed on a map for reference is called
   A. shape file   C. matrix
   B. grid   D. geo-reference

   6._____

7. The intersection of x and y axis in the map projected coordinate system refers to
   A. point in east direction
   B. point in Equator
   C. origin of the location
   D. none of the above

   7._____

8. Google Maps Image API allows
   A. embedding a static Google Maps image into web page
   B. creating a gallery of maps
   C. map colorization
   D. map simulation

9. The procedure for estimating the value of properties at unsampled locations is called
   A. geographic estimation
   B. spatial Interpolation
   C. spatial sampling
   D. location estimation

10. ESRI product that integrates traditional GIS with cloud platform is
    A. EsriCloud
    B. ArcGIS Online
    C. ArcGIS server
    D. ArcView

11. Which of the following is not a GIS package?
    A. QGIS
    B. ArcGIS
    C. NetScape
    D. Idrisi32

12. AM/FM GIS refers to
    A. GIS tools that allow users to digitize, manage and analyze land record data
    B. GIS software that allows utility users to digitize, manage and analyze their utility network data
    C. GIS software that allows users to digitize, manage and analyze population data
    D. none of the above

13. Which of the following is a true statement?
    A. Vector data resolution has to be enhanced for viewing it properly
    B. Vector data topology is dynamic
    C. Vector data can be represented in its original resolution
    D. Continuous data is represented very effectively in vector format

14. Digital Elevation Model (DEM) represents a
    A. terrain surface in 3D
    B. shapefile
    C. TIGER format
    D. water surface

15. Which one of the following is an example of coverage data in GIS?
    A. Shape file
    B. Geospatial database
    C. Raster
    D. Vector

16. Transformation of Earth's model from 3D to 2D is known as
    A. map projection
    B. map conversion
    C. cartography
    D. elevation

    16._____

17. What is E00 file?
    A. A file containing latitudes and longitudes of different landscapes
    B. A file containing locations of different points of interest in the world
    C. A Google Maps data file
    D. ESRI's file format to import and export ArcInfo data files

    17._____

18. TIGER is an abbreviation of
    A. Topological Intelligence and Geographic Environment and Referencing
    B. Topologically Integrated Geographic Environment and Referencing
    C. Topologically Integrated Geographic Encoding and Referencing
    D. Topologically Integrated Geo-spatial Environment and Referencing

    18._____

19. TIGER format was previously known as
    A. DIME
    B. DIVE
    C. E00
    D. Shapefile

    19._____

20. GRASS is a GIS tool that stands for
    A. Geographic Resources Almanac Support System
    B. Geo-spatial Review Analysis Support System
    C. Geographic Resources Analysis Support System
    D. Geographic Resources Alternate Simple System

    20._____

21. A vector based representation of physical land made up of irregularly distributed nodes and lines with 3D coordinates is known as
    A. Digital Elevation Model
    B. Triangulated Irregular Network
    C. Continuous data
    D. TIGER

    21._____

22. A grid-based GIS coordinate system that specifies locations on Earth's surface is called
    A. Universal Transverse Mercator (UTM)
    B. North American Datum (NAD)
    C. map projection
    D. tessellation

    22._____

23. A Digital Earth Reference Model (DERM) refers to a
    A. geospatial platform that acts as a reference model to use geo-referenced information
    B. geospatial framework that allows importing and exporting of vector data
    C. simulation of earth's surface in 3D
    D. none of the above

    23._____

24. In GIS, coverage refers to
    A. mapping of multiple aspects in a single representation
    B. mapping of one aspect of data in space
    C. types of data in a system
    D. none of the above

25. GeoTIFF is a file format that
    A. embeds geo-coded information into raster file
    B. embeds image registration information directory into raster file
    C. embeds geo-coded information into vector file
    D. imports or exports geo-spatial data

KEY (CORRECT ANSWERS)

1.	A		11.	C
2.	D		12.	B
3.	C		13.	C
4.	A		14.	A
5.	C		15.	A
6.	B		16.	A
7.	C		17.	D
8.	A		18.	C
9.	B		19.	A
10.	B		20.	C

21.	B
22.	A
23.	A
24.	B
25.	B

TEST 4

DIRECTIONS: Each question or incomplete statement is followed by several suggested answers of completions. Select the one that BEST answers the question or complete the statement. PRINT THE LETTER OF THE CORRECT ANSWER IN THE SPACE AT THE RIGHT.

1. Google Directions API refers to a(n) 1._____
   A. service that directs and helps in map usage
   B. API used to return distance between origin and destination
   C. service that calculates directions between locations
   D. API to follow location of a particular user

2. Which form of representation does a paper map use? 2._____
   A. Analogue
   B. Binary
   C. Decimal
   D. Digital

3. Which of the following statements are true? 3._____
   A. GISs are incapable of getting field data into their databases
   B. GISs are incapable of getting satellite imagery into their databases
   C. GISs are incapable of getting attribute data into their databases
   D. GISs are incapable of storing all types of map data in the ordinary flat file structure

4. Data about data is called 4._____
   A. nested data
   B. meta data
   C. world wide web
   D. catalog

5. A digitizing tablet and mouse are examples of 5._____
   A. infrastructure of GIS
   B. input devices used in digitizing
   C. output devices used in digitizing
   D. techniques of digitizing

6. The origin of a raster grid in IDRISI is 6._____
   A. lower right corner
   B. upper right corner
   C. upper left corner
   D. random

7. To embed a Google Map on a web page without any JavaScript or page loading, which of the following APIs can be used? 7._____
   A. Street View API
   B. Google Maps Image API
   C. Google Places API
   D. Static Maps API

8. The division of a two-dimensional area into polygonal tiles, or a three-dimensional area into polyhedral blocks, is known as
   A. projection
   B. tessellation
   C. interpolation
   D. alleviation

9. A federally mandated framework of spatial data that refers to U.S is known as
   A. National Spatial Data Infrastructure (NSDI)
   B. North American Datum (NAD)
   C. American National Standards Institute (ANSI)
   D. Environmental Systems Research Institute (ESRI)

10. Batch geo-coding refers to the process of geo-coding
    A. one address at a time
    B. multiple address at a time
    C. addresses in Google Maps API
    D. addresses in standard format

11. The process of determining exact position with GPS and recording location of an object at regular intervals as well as allowing the location to show on map is known as
    A. geo-tagging
    B. geo-coding
    C. geo-caching
    D. geo-tracking

12. Controlling of advertisements within maps is done with the help of
    A. Google Places API
    B. Google Maps API for Business
    C. Google Maps Web Services
    D. Google Directions API

13. A Google Maps API responsible for returning distance based on recommended route between start and end point is known as
    A. Google Distance Matrix API
    B. Google Distance Calculation API
    C. Google Directions API
    D. Google Elevation API

14. If we want to determine the depth locations of an ocean floor, we'll use which of the following APIs?
    A. Google Directions API
    B. Google Distance Matrix API
    C. Google Elevation API
    D. Google Places API

15. Google Street View Image API allows
    A. embedding a static StreetView Panorama on our web page
    B. embedding a dynamic StreetView Panorama using JavaScript
    C. showing simulation of StreetView Panorama
    D. none of the above

16. To overlay, compare or cross-analyze two maps in a GIS, both maps must be
    A. in digital form
    B. in the same map projection
    C. at the same equivalent scale
    D. on the same coordinate system

16._____

17. In GIS, property of connectivity is also known as
    A. proximity
    B. neighborhood
    C. topology
    D. boolean identity

17._____

18. Using a smaller cell size in a raster GIS will result in
    A. more storage required
    B. less storage required
    C. a greater range of values
    D. less resolution

18._____

19. Examples of points, lines and areas in context of GIS data are
    A. wetlands, ponds and parks
    B. oil wells, pipelines and fields
    C. trees, loggers and lumber mills
    D. GPS points, big businesses and land covers

19._____

20. Which of the following types of remote sensing would be best suited for locating deforestation?
    A. Thermal infrared
    B. Microwave
    C. Radar
    D. Color infrared

20._____

21. Three models that have been used by geodesy and cartography are
    A. ellipsoid, sphere and geoid
    B. circle, cone and cylinder
    C. ellipsoid, spheroid and geode
    D. prolate spheroid, oblate cylindroid and geoid

21._____

22. An oblate ellipsoid is a(n)
    A. circle rotated about its major axis
    B. ellipse rotated about its shorter axis
    C. map projection
    D. ellipse rotated about its longer axis

22._____

23. Which is NOT true of the UTM system?
    A. The earth is divided into 60 UTM zones, 6 degrees wide
    B. Zones are numbered west to east, starting at 180 degrees west
    C. Each zone is drawn on a Transverse Mercator projection, centered on the central meridian
    D. The UTM system covers the whole planet in one consistent metric system of coordinates

23._____

24. Tobler's first law of geography states that
    A. any area of interest will always lie at the intersection of at least two maps or images
    B. everything is related to everything else, but near things are more related than distant things
    C. resolution of raster data is directly related to cell size
    D. none of the above

25. Web Map Server Configuration refers to
    A. GIS tool
    B. a set of interface specifications that provides uniform access by Web clients to maps rendered by map servers on the Internet
    C. network protocols
    D. none of the above

KEY (CORRECT ANSWERS)

1. C
2. A
3. D
4. B
5. B

6. C
7. D
8. B
9. A
10. B

11. D
12. B
13. A
14. C
15. A

16. A
17. C
18. A
19. B
20. D

21. C
22. B
23. D
24. B
25. B

EXAMINATION SECTION
TEST 1

DIRECTIONS: Each question or incomplete statement is followed by several suggested answers or completions. Select the one that BEST answers the question or completes the statement. *PRINT THE LETTER OF THE CORRECT ANSWER IN THE SPACE AT THE RIGHT.*

1. A database uses _____ to identify information.   1.____

    A. record numbers
    B. register addresses
    C. field names
    D. directories

2. _____ could be added to a database in order to increase the number of search and access points available to a user.   2.____

    A. Subject discriptors
    B. Partitions
    C. Term authority lists
    D. Call programs

3. The central idea behind the management of a database is   3.____

    A. procedural and nonprocedural interfaces
    B. minimal redundancy and minimal storage space
    C. physical data independence
    D. the separation of data description and data manipulation

4. Which of the following is NOT a type of query language operator used in database searches?   4.____

    A. Object-oriented
    B. Logical
    C. Relational
    D. Mathematical

5. When accessing a record in an indexed file, which of the following steps would be performed FIRST?   5.____

    A. Accessing the index
    B. Disk access to the record or bucket
    C. Data transfer from disk to main program memory
    D. Relative address conversion to absolute address

6. A database management system (DBMS) that employs a hierarchy, but may relate each lower-level data element to more than one parent element, is classified specifically as a(n) _____ DBMS.   6.____

    A. object-oriented
    B. network
    C. relational
    D. aggregational

7. A value-added field might be added to a database in order to   7.____

    A. standardize field formats
    B. estimate the disk capacity for a full database
    C. provide indexing consistency
    D. improve retrieval

8. Each of the following disks is a type of direct-access disk-storage system EXCEPT

   A. magnetic disk
   B. floppy
   C. moving-capstan
   D. fixed-head

9. In determining an appropriate file organization, three principal factors must be considered.
   Which of the following is NOT one of these factors?

   A. Volatility
   B. Conversion
   C. Activity
   D. Size

10. A _____ file is used to update or modify data in a master file.

    A. descriptor
    B. transaction
    C. secondary
    D. conversion

11. Which of the following steps in designing and using a database would be performed FIRST?

    A. Selecting a name for the file
    B. Deciding the form into which information should be stored
    C. Data definition
    D. Defining the type of data to be stored in each field

12. Each of the following is an advantage associated with the use of a DBMS over a flat-file system EXCEPT

    A. fewer storage requirements
    B. better data integrity
    C. lower software costs
    D. lower operating costs

13. Memory storage space that is not directly addressable by processor instructions, but by specialized I/O instructions, is called

    A. allocated memory
    B. secondary storage
    C. internal storage
    D. main memory

14. Which of the following is NOT a disadvantage associated with sequential file processing?

    A. Master files must be sorted into key field sequence.
    B. Files are only current immediately after an update.
    C. Files are difficult to design.
    D. Transaction files must be stored in the same key.

15. When data is updated in some, but not all, of the files in which it appears, _____ has occurred.

    A. data confusion
    B. data dependence
    C. cross-keying
    D. data redundancy

16. The MOST common medium for direct-access storage is

    A. optical disk
    B. magnetic tape
    C. hard card
    D. magnetic disk

17. The purpose of *hashing* is to

    A. discover an unpartitioned sector onto which data may be written
    B. determine a schedule by which batch-processed data may be submitted to the computer
    C. create a buffer delay between data entry and output during interactive processing
    D. convert the key field value for a record to the address of the record on a file

18. What is the term for the description of a specific set of data corresponding to a model of an enterprise, which is obtained by using a particular data description language?

    A. Schema
    B. Descriptor
    C. Object instance
    D. Conceptualization

19. In a sequential file, records are arranged in sequence according to one or more

    A. query languages
    B. column numbers
    C. key fields
    D. hash marks

20. Which of the following is NOT a mathematical query language operator used in database searches?

    A. +
    B. >=
    C. ^
    D. /

21. In _____ file organization, the cost per each transaction processed remains about the same as the percent of records accessed on a file increases.

    A. sequential
    B. hashed
    C. indexed sequential
    D. random

22. For more complex data types, such as those used in multimedia applications, what type of DBMS would be MOST useful?

    A. Hierarchical
    B. Relational
    C. Object-oriented
    D. Network

23. When determining how many generations of a file to retain in a database, the PRIMARY factor is usually

    A. hardware capabilities
    B. storage space
    C. whether files are keyed or indexed
    D. probability of need to access old data for recovery purposes

24. When data is transferred from a user program to secondary storage, it first passes through

    A. program private memory
    B. file system buffers
    C. I/O buffers
    D. program code

25. In order to maintain files in a database, each of the following operations is typically required EXCEPT

    A. balancing index trees
    B. altering the file system's directory
    C. changing field widths
    D. adding fields to records

KEY (CORRECT ANSWERS)

1.	C	11.	B
2.	A	12.	C
3.	D	13.	B
4.	A	14.	C
5.	A	15.	A
6.	B	16.	D
7.	D	17.	D
8.	C	18.	A
9.	B	19.	C
10.	B	20.	B

21. D
22. C
23. D
24. D
25. B

TEST 2

DIRECTIONS: Each question or incomplete statement is followed by several suggested answers or completions. Select the one that BEST answers the question or completes the statement. *PRINT THE LETTER OF THE CORRECT ANSWER IN THE SPACE AT THE RIGHT.*

1. An installation has two tape drives and one disk drive. An application program requires access to three sequential files: an old master file, a transaction file, and an updated master file.
   Typically, the _____ file should be stored on the disk. 1.____

   A. old master
   B. transaction
   C. updated master
   D. both versions of the master

2. The purpose of *record blocking* is to 2.____

   A. allow multiple records to be brought into main memory in a single access to secondary storage
   B. create the illusion of a *virtual device* for the program until the spooler copies a record to the real device
   C. allocate more free buffer space to a file prior to run-unit determination
   D. offload responsibilities for building data paths from the CPU

3. Entries in a database's secondary key tables (index files), which tell the computer where a data is stored on the disk, are 3.____

   A. logical records   B. data addresses
   C. physical records   D. secondary keys

4. Of the types of file organization below, which involves the LOWEST volatility? 4.____

   A. Direct   B. Sequential
   C. Master-keyed   D. Indexed

5. Typically each of the following elements is defined during the *data definition* process EXCEPT 5.____

   A. field types   B. field names
   C. number of columns   D. width of fields

6. A database's master index contains 6.____

   A. the key values for an indexed sequential file
   B. the machine code for every field in a given set of records
   C. the logical record for every randomly-accessed file
   D. each field's physical location on a disk pack

7. Which of the following types of information would MOST likely be stored in a logic field? 7.____

   A. Calendar month/day/year
   B. A patient or customer's mailing address
   C. Numbers that may later be involved in some mathematical calculations
   D. The designation of an employee's status is hourly or salaried

8. When determining how frequently a sequential master file should be updated, each of the following factors should be considered EXCEPT

   A. activity ratio
   B. rate of data change
   C. storage space
   D. urgency for current data

9. Which of the following programs is a file manager, rather than a DBMS?

   A. Q&A   B. FoxPro   C. Approach   D. Paradox

10. Which of the following is NOT an advantage associated with the use of indexed file processing?

    A. No need for hashing algorithm
    B. Random access is faster than direct processing
    C. Can function with applications required for both sequential and direct processing
    D. Access to specific records faster than sequential processing

11. Of the query language operators listed below, which is mathematical?

    A. AND   B. SUB   C. <   D. SQRT(N)

12. A collection of records may sometimes be structured as a file on secondary storage, rather than as a data structure in main memory.
    Which of the following is NOT a possible reason for this?

    A. Permanence of storage
    B. Security concerns
    C. Size of collection
    D. Selective access requirements

13. What is the term for the disk rotation time needed for the physical record to pass under read/write heads?

    A. Transaction time
    B. Latency time
    C. Head displacement time
    D. Transfer time

14. The subset of a database schema required by a particular application program is referred to as a(n)

    A. root
    B. user's view
    C. logical structure
    D. node

15. Which of the following steps in designing and using a database would be performed LAST?

    A. Defining the type of data that will be stored in each field
    B. Assigning field names
    C. Data definition
    D. Defining the width of alphanumeric and numeric fields

16. What type of database structure organizes data in the form of two-dimensional tables?

    A. Relational
    B. Network
    C. Logical
    D. Hierarchical

17. What is the term for the specific modules that are capable of reading and writing buffer contents on devices?   17.____

    A. Spoolers B. Device handlers
    C. I/O managers D. Memory allocators

18. Each of the following is a disadvantage associated with the use of a DBMS EXCEPT   18.____

    A. extensive conversion costs
    B. possible wide distribution of data losses and damage
    C. reduced data security
    D. start-up costs

19. _____ decisions about a database begin after a feasibility study and continue to be refined throughout the design and creation process.   19.____

    A. Procedural B. Structural
    C. Conversion D. Content

20. Each of the following is an advantage associated with direct file processing EXCEPT   20.____

    A. ability to update several files at the same time
    B. no need for separate transaction files
    C. files do not have to be sorted into key field sequence
    D. fewer storage space required than for sequential processing

21. The core of any file management system accesses secondary storage through   21.____

    A. the I/O manager B. file system buffers
    C. relative addressing D. key access

22. Each of the following is a responsibility typically belonging to a file system EXCEPT   22.____

    A. maintaining directories
    B. interfacing the CPU with a secondary storage device
    C. establishing paths for data flow between main memory and secondary storage
    D. buffering data for delivery to the CPU or secondary devices

23. In a hierarchical database, there are several phone numbers belonging to a single address.   23.____
    This is an example of

    A. vector data aggregate B. data dependence
    C. data confusion D. data redundancy

24. A DBMS might access the data dictionary for each of the following purposes EXCEPT   24.____

    A. change the description of a data field
    B. to determine if a data element already exists before adding
    C. request and deliver information from the database to the user
    D. determine what application programs can access what data elements

25. _____ would MOST likely be stored in a memo field. 25.____
   A. A revisable listing of symptoms specific to a particular ailment
   B. The designation of a patient's gender (male/female)
   C. A patient's billing number
   D. The date of a patient's last visit

KEY (CORRECT ANSWERS)

1.	B	11.	D
2.	A	12.	B
3.	A	13.	B
4.	B	14.	B
5.	C	15.	D
6.	A	16.	A
7.	D	17.	B
8.	C	18.	C
9.	A	19.	B
10.	B	20.	D

21. A
22. B
23. A
24. C
25. A

EXAMINATION SECTION
TEST 1

DIRECTIONS: Each question or incomplete statement is followed by several suggested answers or completions. Select the one that BEST answers the question or completes the statement. *PRINT THE LETTER OF THE CORRECT ANSWER IN THE SPACE AT THE RIGHT.*

1. The graphic symbol shown at the right is used by cartographers and other personnel as a signal during the process of compiling a map. What specification does it indicate?

    A. Wrong-reading position
    B. Scribing details
    C. Negative form
    D. Line style

2. What type of cartographic recording medium is the most significant used in map reproduction?

    A. Blue-sensitive emulsions
    B. Color film
    C. Orthochromatic emulsions
    D. Panchromatic emulsions

3. The GREATEST advantage associated with the use of the CIE color system in cartography is that

    A. it is based on the characteristics of subtractive pigments
    B. equal distances in the color solid represent equal visual distances
    C. any color may be precisely specified in physical terms
    D. it is based on a wheel of only ten major hues

4. Which of the following steps in using a pre-sensitized peel-coat mask would be performed FIRST?

    A. The applicator block is soaked with etch solution.
    B. The exposed side is placed face down in developer.
    C. Remaining material is blotted from the surface of the peel coat.
    D. Developer is rinsed from the surface the peel coat

5. What is the term for a polyester-based material overlaid with a photographically opaque red, orange, or yellow membrane?

    A. Control block
    B. Photo-polymer
    C. Scribecoat
    D. Strip mask

6. The MAJOR difficulty involved in mapping a statistical surface with hachures is that

    A. their effectiveness depends upon the hue of the ink
    B. profiles portrayed by this method are not accurate
    C. although slope is their basis, they cannot be practically measured from the map
    D. their application is restricted to showing gradients on a land surface

7. In USGS 7 1/2 minute quadrangles, the color brown is traditionally used for   7____

   A. grid ticks   B. contour lines
   C. railroads   D. forest tint

8. After a map has gone through production and reached its final form, a cartographer duffs   8____
   a negative with brown opaquing fluid. The cartographer is correcting for

   A. white spots   B. missing line work
   C. black spots   D. superimposition

9. Each of the following is a way in which lettering can effectively serve as a locative device   9____
   EXCEPT by

   A. indicating the orientation and length of linear phenomena such as mountain ranges
   B. designating the form and extent of areas such as regions or states
   C. referring to point locations such as cities
   D. spacing to indicate volumetric data such as population differentials

10. In computer cartography, polygons are usually digitized as   10____

    A. strings   B. stacks   C. chains   D. rings

Questions 11-15.

DIRECTIONS: Questions 11 through 15 refer to the figure following, a diagram of several equivalent world map projections. Place the letter that corresponds to each projection in the space at the right of the projection's name.

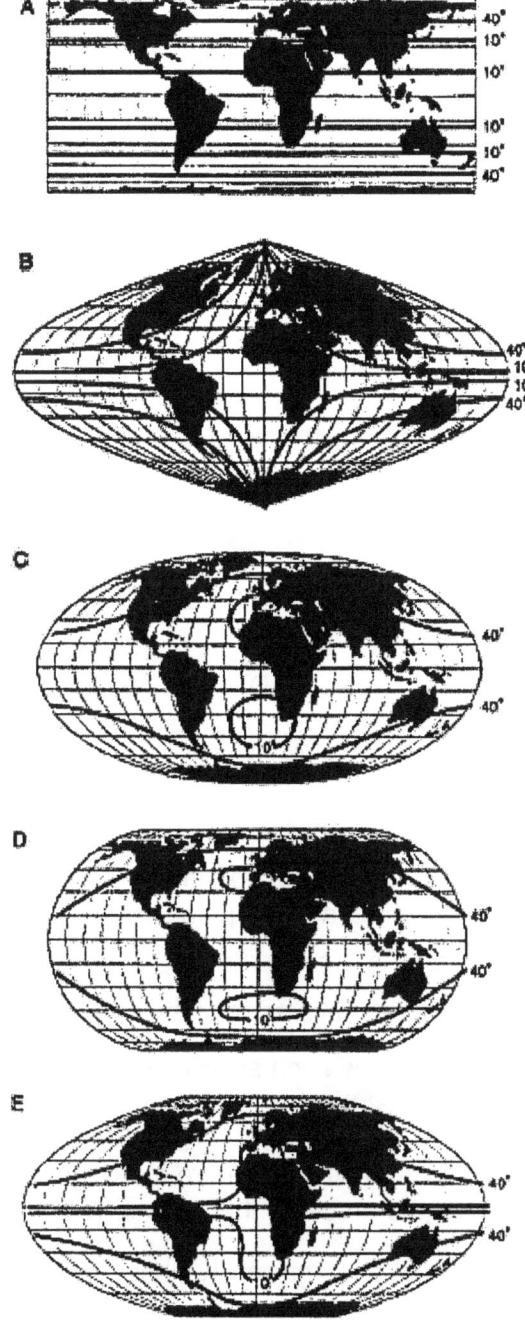

11. Flat polar quartic projection 11.____

12. Mollweide's projection 12.____

13. Cylindrical equal-area with standard parallels at 30N and S latitude 13.____

14. Sinusoidal projection 14.____

15. Eckert's No. IV projection 15.____

16. In computer cartography, raster technology is MOST appropriate for portraying 16.____
    A. quantitative differences among areal units
    B. contour threading
    C. clipping and simple geometric transformations
    D. the change in direction between successive linear boundary segments

17. The graphic symbol shown at the right is used by cartographers and other personnel as a signal during the process of compiling a map. What specification does it indicate? 17.____
    A. Diazo processing   B. Stick-up style
    C. Half-tone processing   D. Paint mask details

18. In computer cartography, the PRIMARY difficulty involved in the conversion of grid data into Freeman codes is 18.____
    A. the length of diagonals and the primary directions is essentially incompatible
    B. Freeman codes cannot be run-length encoded
    C. the difficulty in representing a line as a sequence of numerical codes
    D. the introduction of differing data structures

19. Graduated symbol maps are most useful in each of the following situations EXCEPT 19.____
    A. for symbolizing totals of quantities such as tonnage and costs
    B. if the cartographer does not wish to show relative sizes of each individual statistical quantity
    C. when point data exist in close proximity but are too large in aggregate number
    D. for representing the aggregate amounts that refer to relatively large territories

20. In general, a camera used for aerial photography will have to be capable of exposure times down to _____ second. 20.____
    A. 1/500   B. 1/1000   C. 1/5000   D. 1/10,000

21. The numeric label attached to a line or point on a cartographic plane is known as a(n) 21.____
    A. cursor   B. feature code
    C. node   D. fiducial mark

22. Which of the following steps involved in digitizing a map would be performed FIRST? 22.____
    A. The selection of control points
    B. Interactively entering the world coordinates of control points
    C. Deriving a coordinate system for the map
    D. Integration of data into computer mapping software

23. What kind of cartographic data scaling system adds the information of distance between ranks to the description of kind and rank? 23____

    A. Nominal B. Interval C. Ratio D. Ordinal

24. Small circles are MOST effectively drawn on a map manuscript with a 24____

    A. border pen
    B. beam compass
    C. double ruling pen with an interior adjusting wheel
    D. drop compass

25. On a map, the different types of roads in an area (interstate, state, county, etc.) are mapped as _____ data. 25____

    A. ordinal   B. interval-ratio
    C. nominal   D. area

KEY (CORRECT ANSWERS)

1.	A	11.	E
2.	C	12.	C
3.	C	13.	A
4.	B	14.	B
5.	D	15.	D
6.	C	16.	A
7.	B	17.	C
8.	A	18.	A
9.	D	19.	B
10.	C	20.	B

21. B
22. C
23. B
24. D
25. A

TEST 2

DIRECTIONS: Each question or incomplete statement is followed by several suggested answers or completions. Select the one that BEST answers the question or completes the statement. *PRINT THE LETTER OF THE CORRECT ANSWER IN THE SPACE AT THE RIGHT.*

1. For mapping place data, the MOST commonly used point symbol is

   A. graduated sphere
   B. circle segment
   C. graduated circle
   D. block pile

2. The graphic symbol shown at the right is used by cartographers and other personnel as a signal during the process of compiling a map. What specification does it indicate?

   A. Blue key style
   B. Translucent details
   C. Emulsion-to-emulsion contact processing
   D. Positive form

3. If geographical variables are mapped using a nominal scale, the averaging method used will be the

   A. arithmetic mean
   B. geometric mean
   C. mode
   D. median

4. The earth's irregular shape which takes into account variations in gravity is known as the

   A. geoid
   B. globe
   C. ellipsoid
   D. spheroid

5. Overlay proofs are often not satisfactory for making proofs *of* color (as opposed to *in* color), primarily because

   A. they do not show a range of color that is broad enough
   B. it is almost impossible to avoid a crabbed exposure
   C. they often cause blurring of linear elements
   D. the various layers of translucent material cause reflections

6. The limit of reliable estimation of any scale is known as its

   A. frequency distribution
   B. resolution
   C. termination
   D. vanishing point

7. The relative lightness or darkness of a mark is described in terms of

   A. hue
   B. value
   C. tone
   D. contrast

8. Each of the following is a conformal projection in common use by cartographers EXCEPT

   A. Lambert's conformal conic with two standard parallels
   B. Mercator's
   C. the gnomonic
   D. the stereographic

9. The MOST common error associated with the use of pictorial symbols in mapping is that

   A. the symbols are not easily distinguishable from one another
   B. they are used to map linear relationships
   C. too few symbols of roughly equivalent size are used
   D. the symbols are not graduated correctly for the data they represent

10. The removal of high-frequency components from data by the application of moving averages or other filtering processes is known as

    A. conforming
    B. smoothing
    C. stringing
    D. digitizing

11. Any trace of the intersection of a horizontal plane with a statistical surface is a(n)

    A. oblique trace
    B. isarithm
    C. derivation
    D. choropleth

12. If the scale of a map is known to be 1/25,000, what is the map distance which corresponds to a ground distance of 2 km?

    A. 2.5 cm
    B. 8.0 cm
    C. 25 cm
    D. 1 m

13. The absolute orientation process, performed on two projected images of an aerial photograph, will yield each of the following EXCEPT

    A. the orientation of the plot
    B. radial displacements of taller features
    C. the position of the plot within the coordinate frame of reference
    D. a scale factor for the model

14. The focal length of an aerial camera is 0.5 feet. If the camera is used from a height of 10,000 feet above the datum, what is the scale ratio of the image?

    A. 1:5,000
    B. 1:10,000
    C. 1:20,000
    D. 1:200,000

15. In computer cartography, two nodes in a graphic representation of a data structure are linked by a line known as a(n)

    A. edge
    B. chain
    C. queue
    D. string

16. For large and medium scale maps without a grid, the spacing of the master grid lines should be about _____ mm if the graticule is to be plotted by manual methods.

    A. 5-10
    B. 15-30
    C. 20-50
    D. 30-75

17. An isarithmic map resulting from place data is described as a(n) _____ map.

    A. dasymetric
    B. isometric
    C. choroplethic
    D. isoplethic

18. In aerial photography, the phenomenon of _____ is most serious in urban areas over which there are many tall buildings.

    A. parallax
    B. pitch distortion
    C. dead ground
    D. crabbing

19. If geographical variables are mapped using a ratio scale, the index of variation used will be the

   A. standard deviation
   B. arithmetic mean
   C. variation ratio
   D. decile range

20. What would be the grid separation (km) on a map with a scale of 1/5,000?

   A. 0.01   B. 0.1   C. 1.0   D. 10.0

21. In an aerial scanning device, the ground distance covered for any time increment during scanning increases toward the edge of the scan line. This type of distortion is described as

   A. one-dimensional relief
   B. resolution cell size variation
   C. flight parameter
   D. tangential scale

22. The two sets of circles shown above are nested graduated circles prepared from the same data. The set on the right could best be described as

   A. scaled proportionally in relation to area
   B. ordinal place data
   C. psychologically scaled to compensate for underestimation
   D. range-graded from mimetic to arbitrary symbolization

23. Which of the following is NOT a *perceptual* primary color?

   A. Brown   B. White   C. Magenta   D. Yellow

24. For cartographers, the principle advantage of raster technologies and data structures is

   A. the ease with which network linkages are established
   B. their low volume of required data
   C. the ease with which map projection transformations are performed
   D. their simplicity

25. For mapmaking, which of the following base materials is generally LEAST flexible?

   A. Drawing paper
   B. Polyvinyl plastic
   C. Tracing paper
   D. Polyester plastic

KEY (CORRECT ANSWERS)

1.	C	11.	B
2.	D	12.	B
3.	C	13.	B
4.	A	14.	C
5.	D	15.	A
6.	B	16.	C
7.	B	17.	B
8.	C	18.	C
9.	A	19.	A
10.	B	20.	B

21.	D
22.	C
23.	C
24.	D
25.	B

EXAMINATION SECTION
TEST 1

DIRECTIONS: Each question or incomplete statement is followed by several suggested answers or completions. Select the one that BEST answers the question or completes the statement. *PRINT THE LETTER OF THE CORRECT ANSWER IN THE SPACE AT THE RIGHT.*

1. A map has a scale of 1:75,000. On this map, one kilometer would be represented by

   A. 7.5 mm   B. 33 mm   C. 1.25 cm   D. 1.33 cm

   1_____

2. Errors in choroplethic mapping commonly result from attempts to portray each of the following EXCEPT

   A. significant boundary lines for the distribution
   B. an overview of the distribution
   C. arithmetic progressions within classes
   D. the geographical positions of tabular values from the distribution

   2_____

3. Which of the following is NOT a characteristic of the UPS grid system?

   A. Grid north is parallel to true north along the 0° meridian.
   B. The 2 million-m easting coincides with the 0°-180° meridian line.
   C. Zones are divided into 50,000-m squares.
   D. Each circular polar zone is divided in half by the 0°-180° meridian.

   3_____

4. What Thematic Mapper (TM) band is used for the aerial discrimination of rock formations?
   Band _____ micrometers.

   A. 1; 0.45 to 0.52   B. 3; 0.63 to 0.69
   C. 5; 1.55 to 1.75   D. 6; 10.4 to 12.

   4_____

5. The graphic symbols shown at the right are used by cartographers and other personnel as signals during the process of compiling a map. What verbal suggestion is indicated by symbol number 1, the solid line?

   A. Refer to
   B. Use for
   C. Further processing on
   D. Use as underlay

   5_____

6. Each of the following is an element of isarithmic mapping EXCEPT the

   A. number of control points
   B. gradient assumed
   C. angle at which the planes intersect the datum
   D. location of the control points

   6_____

7. The distance between the principal points of two adjacent prints in a series of vertical aerial photographs is known as the

   A. parameter
   B. matrix
   C. photobase
   D. orthophotograph

8. The point on the plane of an aerial photograph located by the extension of a vertical line through the center of the camera lens is known as the

   A. nadir
   B. median
   C. fiducial mark
   D. geographic center

9. Which of the following is NOT a rule of thumb for map lettering?

   A. Names should be letter spaced as little as possible.
   B. Disoriented lettering should be set on a curve, rather than in a straight line.
   C. Names should be entirely on land or on water.
   D. Where the continuity of names and other map data, such as lines and tones, conflicts with the lettering, the names, and not the data, should be interrupted.3

10. After a map has gone through production and reached its final form, a cartographer applies a waxed stripping film to the final product. Most likely, the cartographer is correcting for

    A. black spots
    B. missing line work
    C. underexposure
    D. missing type

11. Directions on a map that are determined by the orientation of the graticule are referred to as _____ directions.

    A. grid
    B. magnetic
    C. scaled
    D. true

12. To portray the internal relationships of an internal data hierarchy on a map, what method of organization should be used?

    A. Subdivisional
    B. Extensional
    C. Stereogrammic
    D. Taxonomic

13. On a map, population densities relative to topographic elevations would be mapped as _____ data.

    A. ordinal
    B. interval-ratio
    C. nominal
    D. point

14. Straightforward applications of the principle of simplification are appropriate for each of the following EXCEPT

    A. linear data sets such as roads or streams
    B. volumetric data sets such as geographical density
    C. areal data sets consisting of numerous small similar sets within a region, such as lakes or islands
    D. including in computer algorithms to evaluate computer generalization schemes

15. By observing the angle that the arc of a great circle makes with the meridian of a starting point, a cartographer determines a(n)

    A. bearing
    B. azimuth
    C. rhumb line
    D. resection

16. What is the term for the attribute of color associated with differences in wavelength?

 A. Brightness B. Intensity
 C. Hue D. Tone

17. What would be the graticule separation (° or ') on a map with a scale of 1/250,000?

 A. 5' B. 30' C. 1° D. 5°

18. What type of cartographic recording medium must be handled and processed in complete darkness?

 A. Blue-sensitive emulsions
 B. Color film
 C. Orthochromatic emulsions
 D. Panchromatic emulsions

19. At what approximate latitude does one degree of parallels measure about 45 statute miles?

 A. 10° B. 30° C. 50° D. 80°

20. For mapmaking, which of the following base materials is considered to have the greatest *foldability*?

 A. Polyester plastic B. Drawing paper
 C. Polyvinyl plastic D. Tracing paper

21. Which of the following is a technique used to conserve computer memory when a cartographic file otherwise would have a large number of unused records?

 A. Aliasing B. Iteration
 C. Hash coding D. Foreshortening

22. In USGS 7 1/2 minute quadrangles, the color magenta is traditionally used for

 A. photo revisions B. urban areas
 C. contour lines D. point symbols

23. The graphic coding of the scaled and/or grouped essential characteristics, comparative significances, and relative positions are processes of cartographic generalization broadly defined as

 A. symbolization B. classification
 C. geocode D. induction

24. A map projection that retains the representation of areas so that all regions in the projection will be represented in correct relative size is described as a(n) _____ projection.

 A. equivalent B. constant
 C. azimuthal D. scaled

25. In flow diagrams used during map production, the graphic symbol indicating the image   25____
    form is situated at the _____ corner of each square in the diagram.

    A. bottom left
    B. bottom right
    C. top left
    D. top right

KEY (CORRECT ANSWERS)

1. D
2. C
3. C
4. D
5. B

6. C
7. C
8. A
9. D
10. D

11. D
12. A
13. B
14. B
15. B

16. C
17. A
18. D
19. C
20. A

21. C
22. A
23. A
24. A
25. D

TEST 2

DIRECTIONS: Each question or incomplete statement is followed by several suggested answers or completions. Select the one that BEST answers the question or completes the statement. *PRINT THE LETTER OF THE CORRECT ANSWER IN THE SPACE AT THE RIGHT.*

Questions 1-5.

DIRECTIONS: Questions 1 through 5 refer to the figure below, a diagram of several common geocoding errors involved in computer cartography. Place the letter that corresponds to error in the space at the right of the error's description.

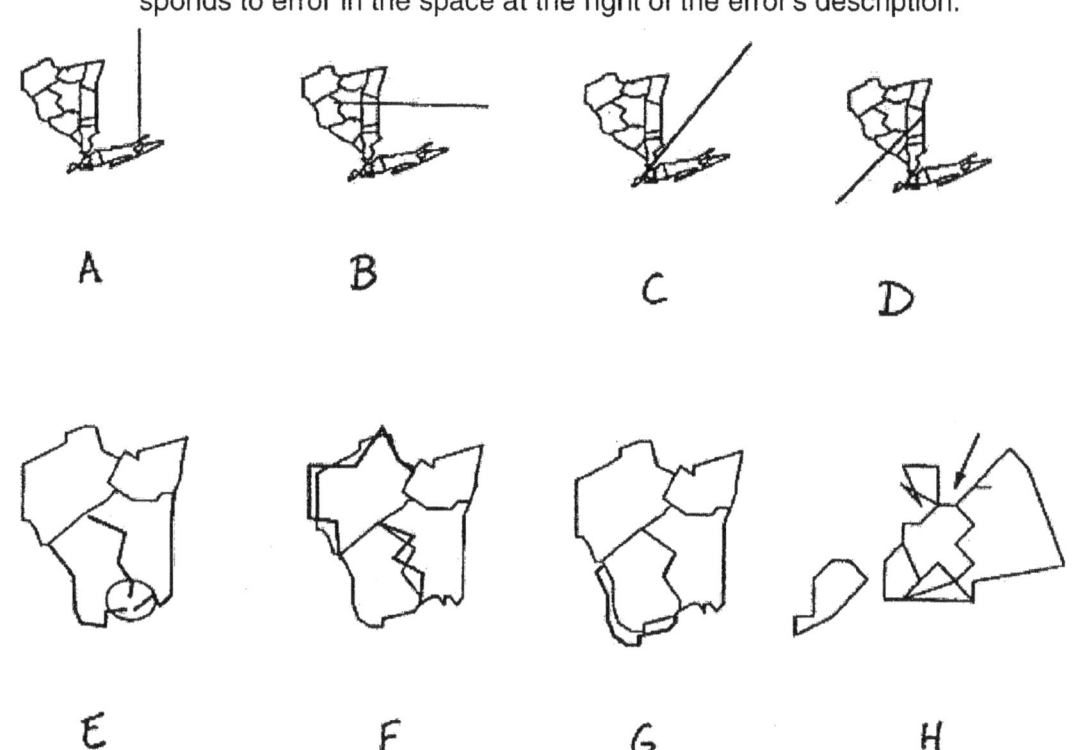

1. Missing chain 1____

2. Spike in y 2____

3. Unsnapped node 3____

4. Duplicate line 4____

5. Slivers 5____

6. If the scale of a map is known to be 1/50,000, what is the ground distance, in km, which corresponds to a map distance of 3.0 cm? 6____

    A. .75   B. 1.5   C. 12   D. 30

7. A cartographer uses line symbols to portray a statistical surface. If the statistical surface is intersected by parallel planes that are at an approximately 45 angle to the datum, the lines of intersection represent 7____

55

A. flow lines B. isarithmic lines
C. oblique traces D. profiles

8. Vertical control in map making is expressed in terms of

 A. densitometry B. gradient
 C. planimetry D. hypsometry

9. The primary problem associated with the design of thematic maps is

 A. the controls imposed by topography
 B. the complex hierarchical decisions involved
 C. difficulties in establishing a proper scale
 D. the numerous categories of data to be mapped

10. Which of the following is NOT an advantage associated with vector technologies and data structures?

 A. The compactness of the vector structure
 B. The inexpensiveness of display technology
 C. Their suitability for representations of lines and polygons
 D. Their reduction of redundancy

11. The agglomeration of areas using ordinal, interval, or ratio scaled data is a form of _____ mapping.

 A. isarithmic B. orthographic
 C. dasymetric D. stereographic

12. According to the ICA, a *small-scale* map is any map with a scale less than

 A. 1/50,000 B. 1/100,000 C. 1/200,000 D. 1/300,000

13. On a map, a(n) _____ pattern occurs if the transformation takes place from the globe to a tangent or an intersecting (secant) plane.

 A. cylindrical B. conical
 C. conformal D. azimuthal

14. Geographical phenomena in which the differences from place to place are transitional, rather than abrupt, are described as

 A. continuous B. graduated
 C. smooth D. flush

15. The graphic symbol shown at the right is used by cartographers and other personnel as a signal during the process of compiling a map. What specification does it indicate?

 A. Line style
 B. Dot screen processing
 C. Photo-etching scribing details
 D. Strip mask details

16. What is the term for the determination of an unknown point on a plane by constructing three angles measured at the unknown point?

A. Resection	B. Transcription
C. Bearing and distance	D. Angular measurement

17. Which of the following computer methods for interpolating point data to a grid uses statistical theory to optimize the interpolation?   17____

   A. Surface-specific point sampling
   B. Kriging
   C. Weighting
   D. Trend projection

18. What kind of cartographic data scaling system differentiates within a class of data on the basis of rank only?   18____

   A. Nominal   B. Interval   C. Ratio   D. Ordinal

19. In aerial photography, the super-wide angle involves a maximum angle of acceptance of approximately _____°.   19____

   A. 57   B. 94   C. 123   D. 180

20. Maps to be used for analyzing, guiding, or recording motion and angular relationships require the use of _____ projections.   20____

   A. azimuthal   B. conformal
   C. conical   D. equivalent

21. The most common problem associated with the use of geometric symbols in mapping is that   21____

   A. they can only represent an extremely limited set of data
   B. the cartographer often attempts to make the symbols associative in nature
   C. the symbols sometimes connote higher than nominally scaled information
   D. the relationships between mapped data are often confused

22. When using a ruling pen, a cartographer should always hold it at a _____° angle to the manuscript surface.   22____

   A. 45   B. 60   C. 70   D. 90

23. During the reproduction process, a cartographer applies two tint screens, the first one rated 50% and the second 30%. What is the approximate percentage of the area covered by the screens that will be inked?   23____

   A. 20%   B. 45%   C. 65%   D. 80%

24. The most important single cause of random error in cartography arises from   24____

   A. slight flexibility in the rigid arms of instruments
   B. the variations in illumination of the scale and plotting sheet, and the effects on a draftsman's eyesight
   C. unequal penetration of divider points
   D. the uncertainty which arises in estimating the distance between the engraved subdivisions of scale

25. What is the term for a printing process in which the image is recessed in the printing surface? 25____

    A. Intaglio
    B. Skeletonizing
    C. Diazo
    D. Fixing

KEY (CORRECT ANSWERS)

1.	H	11.	C
2.	A	12.	C
3.	E	13.	D
4.	G	14.	C
5.	F	15.	A
6.	B	16.	A
7.	C	17.	B
8.	D	18.	D
9.	B	19.	C
10.	B	20.	B

21. C
22. D
23. C
24. D
25. A

EXAMINATION SECTION
TEST 1

DIRECTIONS: Each question or incomplete statement is followed by several suggested answers or completions. Select the one that BEST answers the question or completes the statement. *PRINT THE LETTER OF THE CORRECT ANSWER IN THE SPACE AT THE RIGHT.*

1. An aerial photograph is considered vertical only if the lens is positioned with _____ ° of tilt or less.

    A. 1   B. 3   C. 7   D. 12

2. Which of the following errors associated with digital cartographic data bases is not classified as a *process* error?

    A. Errors due to the transformation of cartographic objects in digital form between data structures
    B. Errors due to an unexpected deviation from cartographic convention
    C. Errors due to changes in scale
    D. Mislocation of features in the three-dimensional geometry of the world

3. What is the term for the practice of depicting lines on a map by means of small, equidistantly spaced dots?

    A. Stippling   B. Aliasing
    C. Rouletting   D. Clefting

4. The primary factors controlling the selection of a representational method for cartographic data include the following EXCEPT the

    A. geographical location of the data
    B. combination of visual variables
    C. types of details to be shown (qualitative or quantitative) and their interrelationships
    D. intended scale of the eventual map

5. In order to determine the arc distance between two points A and B on the globe, each of the following pieces of information is necessary EXCEPT

    A. degrees of longitude between A and B
    B. direction in which the great circle is measured
    C. latitude of B
    D. latitude of A

6. On a single map, point symbols can simultaneously represent up to _____ attributes of range-graded data.

    A. 2   B. 3   C. 4   D. 5

7. In U.S. government aeronautical charts, roads are usually printed in _____ ink.

    A. black   B. magenta   C. cyan   D. yellow

8. Most scales used in small-scale map making are

   A. graphic scales
   B. representative fractions
   C. area scales
   D. verbal statements

9. Each of the following is an important consideration affecting the usefulness of a dot map EXCEPT the

   A. statistical surface
   B. location of the dots
   C. size of the dots
   D. value assigned to a dot

10. Choroplethic mapping often involves class interval series that are irregular or variable. These are typically used when the cartographer wishes to do each of the following EXCEPT

    A. minimize certain error aspects
    B. set class limits such as the mean plus and minus one standard deviation
    C. call attention to various internal characteristics of the distribution
    D. highlight certain elements of the data range that would not be properly dealt with were a constant or regular ascending or descending series being employed

11. Which of the following is NOT one of the basic categories of geographical phenomena?

    A. Areal
    B. Scalar
    C. Place or positional
    D. Volumetric

12. What is the term for the process of transferring cartographic data into computer-readable form?

    A. Geocoding
    B. Plotting
    C. Digitizing
    D. Stringing

13. When it is more realistic to portray an indefinite zone than to show a sharp boundary on a map, a technique known as the _____ may be used to create the desired effect.

    A. hachure
    B. positive mask
    C. vignette
    D. roulette

14. If a map sheet numbering system is arbitrary, the maps are simply numbered serially, beginning in the _____ area.

    A. northwest   B. northeast   C. southwest   D. southeast

15. In computer cartography, what is the term for connected networks which partition space into a set of sub-areas?

    A. Winged segments
    B. Quad trees
    C. Tessellations
    D. Scratch files

16. A map projection that retains the property of angular relations of the compass rose (at each point, the cardinal directions are always 90 apart, and each of the intervening directions is everywhere at the same angle with the cardinal direction) is described as a(n) _____ projection.

    A. orthogonal
    B. uniform
    C. equal-area
    D. conformal

17. Generally, the FIRST step in the cartographic generalization process is

    A. symbolization   B. classification
    C. simplification   D. induction

18. A cartographer determines the location of an unknown point by constructing one angle and one distance from one known point and one known direction. This procedure is commonly known as

    A. linear measurement   B. splining
    C. bearing and distance D. conforming

19. In a flow diagram used during map production, the top right corner of each square in the diagram contains a symbol indicating the

    A. image type   B. method of image formation
    C. image form   D. image position

20. The mathematical function used to divide measurement space into decision regions is the _____ function.

    A. determinant   B. dimensional
    C. exterminant   D. discriminant

21. The basic method for representing a surface by areal symbols in a highly commensurable manner is called _____ mapping.

    A. isometric   B. hypsometric
    C. gnomonic   D. choroplethic

22. A cartographer divides a line into equal parts as follows: a pair of dividers are set to a separation corresponding to a single division, set at one end of the line, and then *walked* along the line, moving each point of the divider in turn. The inevitable error resulting from this method would be categorized as

    A. systematic   B. random
    C. redundant   D. gross

23. In U.S. cartographic applications, the minimum size for legibility of a point symbol viewed from 18 inches is approximately _____ inch.

    A. .003   B. .01   C. .03   D. .07

24. What kind of cartographic data scaling system is employed when distinguishing among a set of things only on the basis of their intrinsic character?

    A. Nominal   B. Interval   C. Ratio   D. Ordinal

25. Which of the following types of contours is used by the USGS as dashed or dotted lines spaced at one-half, one-fourth, or one-fifth the basic contour interval?

    A. Approximate contours   B. Index contours
    C. Supplementary contours   D. Intermediate contours

KEY (CORRECT ANSWERS)

1. B
2. B
3. C
4. B
5. B

6. A
7. D
8. A
9. A
10. B

11. B
12. A
13. C
14. A
15. C

16. D
17. C
18. C
19. A
20. D

21. D
22. A
23. B
24. A
25. C

TEST 2

DIRECTIONS: Each question or incomplete statement is followed by several suggested answers or completions. Select the one that BEST answers the question or completes the statement. *PRINT THE LETTER OF THE CORRECT ANSWER IN THE SPACE AT THE RIGHT.*

1. A cartographer wishes a map viewer to focus on one set of data and, while doing so, to subordinate the rest of the data. What type of hierarchical data organization will be MOST useful for this purpose?

    A. Stereogrammic
    B. Subdivisional
    C. Thematic
    D. Extensional

2. A graphic display of a set of data, which shows the frequency of occurrence of individual measurements or values, is known as a(n)

    A. histogram
    B. pictograph
    C. plotting sheet
    D. coordinate set

3. A cartographer using raster technology elects to store information in an array by using bit planes. If three bit planes are used, how many colors may be stored?

    A. 6   B. 8   C. 16   D. 64

Questions 4-9.

DIRECTIONS: Questions 4 through 9 refer to the plane polar coordinate system shown below.

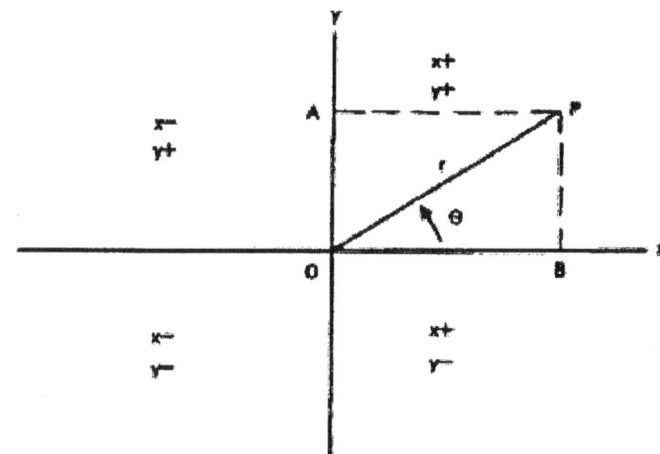

4. The _____ is the point 0 from which measurements are to be made.

    A. abscissa   B. ordinate   C. axis   D. origin

5. The line OA is chosen as the

    A. ordinate   B. origin   C. axis   D. neat line

6. The position of point P is referred to by means of the straight line distance shown, known as

A. slope B. original vector
C. sine D. radius vector

7. The symbol 6 in the figure represents the

   A. axis B. vectorial angle
   C. radius vector D. polar coordinates

8. If the figure above was marked using a Cartesian coordinate system, the line OA would be called the

   A. ordinate B. abscissa C. radius D. y-axis

9. If the figure above was marked using a Cartesian coordinate system, the line OB would be called the

   A. ordinate B. abscissa C. horizon D. x-axis

10. Which of the following is not considered to be a control operating on the process of cartographic generalization?

    A. Scale B. Quality of data
    C. Objective D. Intended user

11. What kind of cartographic data scaling system is considered to be a refinement of the interval scale?

    A. Nominal B. Orthogonal
    C. Ratio D. Ordinal

12. What is the term for a map containing geographical reference information on which attribute data may be plotted for purposes of comparison or geographical coordination?

    A. Plotting sheet B. Drum
    C. Base map D. Scan map

13. The angular orientation of a remote sensing system with respect to a geographical reference system is known as

    A. angularity B. attitude
    C. bearing D. aspect

14. What is the term for the photographic technique in which a solid image is broken up, using a screen, into evenly spaced dots of varying sizes?

    A. Emulsion B. Masking
    C. Halftone D. Resolution

15. On the IMW, or International Map of the World, the 1/1,000,000 map bound by the parallels 48-52 North and by meridians 6°-12° East would have the number

    A. UV5 B. CD60 C. NM32 D. RS13

16. A graticule

    A. always has lines parallel to the ordinate
    B. uses Grid North as an indicator of direction
    C. uses lines for equal values of latitude and longitude
    D. records coordinates as Easting followed by Northing

Questions 17-21.

DIRECTIONS: Questions 17 through 21 refer to the figure below, a diagram of several azimuthal world map projections. Place the letter that corresponds to each projection in the space at the right of the projection's name.

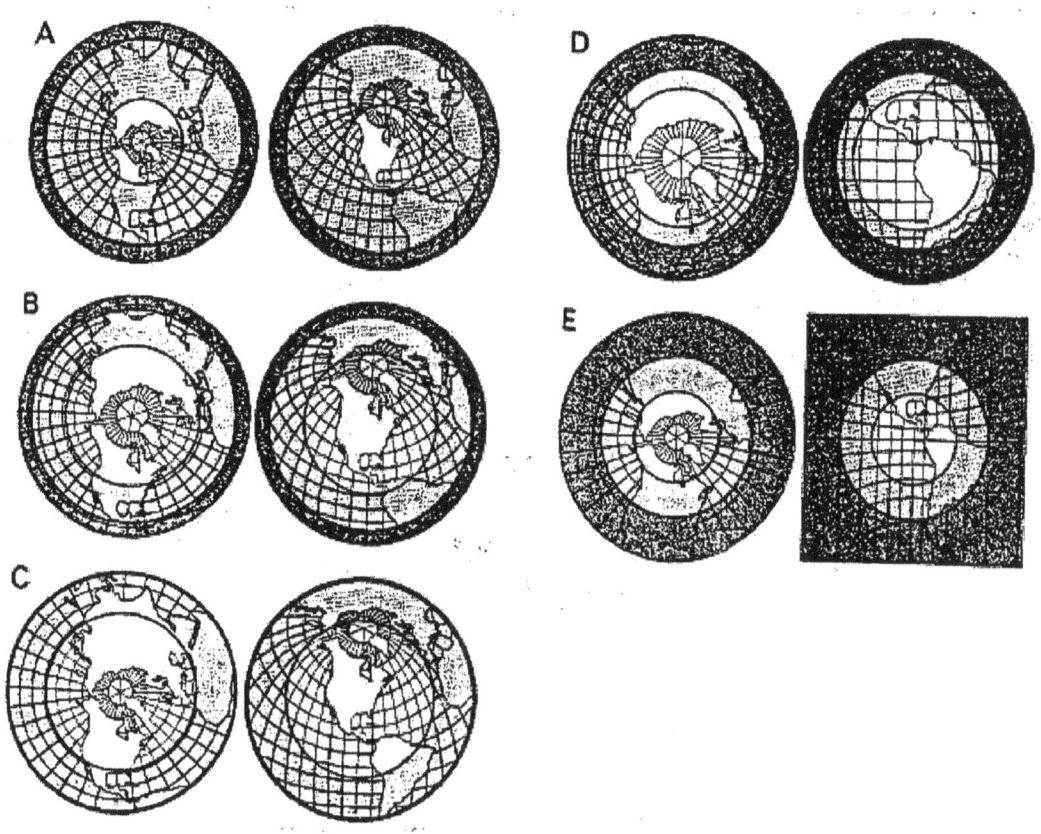

17. Lambert's equal-area   17____

18. Azimuthal equidistant   18____

19. Gnomonic   19____

20. Stereographic   20____

21. Orthographic   21____

22. In the CIE color system, color is specified by each of the following values EXCEPT   22____

    A. tone   B. luminosity
    C. purity   D. dominant wavelength

23. A point common to two or more line segments is called a(n)   23____

    A. intersection   B. node
    C. mote   D. median

24. When the slopes of a statistical surface are considered as values existing at points, the   24____
surface may be portrayed by a line symbol called a(n)

A. isarithm B. profile
C. choropleth D. hachure

25. For a person viewing a map, the visual center is approximately   25____
    A. 5% of the height below the bounding shape or map border
    B. 5% of the height above the bounding shape or map border
    C. within a 2-inch radius of the actual center
    D. at the actual center

KEY (CORRECT ANSWERS)

1. A
2. A
3. B
4. D
5. C

6. D
7. B
8. B
9. A
10. D

11. C
12. C
13. B
14. C
15. C

16. C
17. B
18. C
19. E
20. A

21. D
22. A
23. B
24. D
25. B

EXAMINATION SECTION
TEST 1

DIRECTIONS: Each question or incomplete statement is followed by several suggested answers or completions. Select the one that BEST answers the question or completes the statement. *PRINT THE LETTER OF THE CORRECT ANSWER IN THE SPACE AT THE RIGHT.*

1. What is the term for the ultraviolet-light sensitive chemical compound used to produce cheap blueprints, guideline images, etc.? 1.____

    A. Diazo
    B. Scribecoat
    C. Intaglio
    D. Gum arable

2. In raster technology, the basic graphic unit is the 2.____

    A. node   B. pixel   C. cursor   D. grid cell

3. According to ICA, a *large-scale* map is any map with a scale larger than 3.____

    A. 1/10,000
    B. 1/25,000
    C. 1/50,000
    D. 1/100,000

4. The majority of maps used for instruction and small-scale general maps normally uses what type of projection? 4.____

    A. Conical
    B. Conformal
    C. Cylindrical
    D. Equal-area

5. A map manuscript is commonly referred to as a(n) 5.____

    A. graticule
    B. intaglio
    C. projection
    D. plotting sheet

6. On a single map, point symbols can simultaneously represent up to _____ attributes of nominally scaled data. 6.____

    A. 2   B. 3   C. 4   D. 5

7. The graphic symbol shown at the right is used by cartographers and other personnel as a signal during the process of compiling a map. What specification does it indicate? 7.____

    A. Photomechanical processing
    B. Opaque details
    C. Negative form
    D. Right-reading position

8. Map production is usually controlled by flow diagrams. In these diagrams, the graphic symbol indicating the image position is situated at the _____ corner of each square in the diagram. 8.____

    A. bottom left
    B. bottom right
    C. top left
    D. top right

9. A bearing which intersects meridians at a constant oblique angle is called a(n) 9._____

   A. rhumb line
   B. azimuth
   C. orthogon
   D. great circle

10. Each of the following is a disadvantage associated with the use of vector technologies and data structures EXCEPT 10._____

   A. vector data structures are less intuitively understood by most users of cartographic data
   B. vector data structures offer a poor representation of topological information
   C. the combination by overlay of two vector-based maps is a computationally intensive task
   D. vector-mode devices do not do area fills very well

Questions 11-14.

DIRECTIONS: Questions 11 through 14 refer to the figure below, a diagram of several types of flight parameter distortions induced into scanned cartographic imagery by deviations of the scanning aircraft's attitude. Place the letter corresponding to the illustration of each type of distortion in the space at the right of the corresponding description.

11. Roll distortion 11._____

12. Crab distortion 12._____

13. Scanner image distortion 13._____

14. Pitch distortion 14._____

15. What is the term for the printing or display of different arrays of constant-area dots on graphic output devices in an attempt to produce tones that approximate the variable-area dots of halftone reproduction? 15._____

   A. Blue-lining
   B. Dithering
   C. Intaglio printing
   D. Aliasing

16. Which of the following is NOT a characteristic of the Universal Transverse Mercator (UTM) grid system?

    A. The area of the earth between 84° N and 80° S latitude is divided into north-south columns.
    B. The columns are each 10° of longitude wide.
    C. The rows of quadrilaterals are assigned letters C to X consecutively (with I and O omitted).
    D. Each quadrilateral is divided into 100,000-m zones.

17. What is the term for the lines which enclose all the map detail, and therefore define the limits of the area detailed?

    A. Graticule   B. Neat lines
    C. Sheaf   D. Grid

18. On a map surface, a forest would most likely be shown by

    A. a point symbol   B. a line symbol
    C. ordinal data   D. an area symbol

19. For mapmaking, which of the following base materials has the greatest dimensional stability?

    A. Metal plates laminated with drawing paper
    B. Polyvinyl plastic
    C. Glass plates with lacquered surface
    D. Drawing paper

20. An aerial photograph taken from a height of 10,000 feet shows a broadcasting tower, 100 feet in height, that is located 600 feet from the principal point of the photograph. What is the radial displacement involved in the image of the tower?

    A. .167   B. 1.67   C. 6   D. 60

21. Each of the following would be considered a gross error in measurement and plotting EXCEPT

    A. an incorrect scale reading
    B. an accidental alteration in the setting of instruments
    C. the transposition of numbers in copying
    D. the use of redundant measurements

22. When using a drawing pen, a cartographer should always hold it at a _____° angle to the manuscript surface.

    A. 45   B. 60   C. 70   D. 90

23. Which of the following factors is LEAST likely to affect the appearance of mapped line symbols?

    A. Compactness
    B. Closure
    C. Hue
    D. Brightness contrast

24. The graphic symbol shown at the right is used by cartographers and other personnel as a signal during the process of compiling a map. What specification does it indicate?

24._____

A. Blue key style
B. Strip mask detailing
C. Proof style
D. Diazo print

25. During map design, a cartographer uses an extensional method of creating hierarchical relationships among map data. For which of the following would this method be most useful?

25._____

A. Classifying different types of bedrock or soil
B. Categorizing land use
C. To show territories that have changed hands over time
D. Differentiating between different classes of roads in a road system

KEY (CORRECT ANSWERS)

1. A
2. D
3. B
4. D
5. D

6. C
7. A
8. C
9. A
10. B

11. C
12. D
13. B
14. E
15. B

16. B
17. B
18. D
19. C
20. C

21. D
22. C
23. C
24. B
25. D

TEST 2

DIRECTIONS: Each question or incomplete statement is followed by several suggested answers or completions. Select the one that BEST answers the question or completes the statement. *PRINT THE LETTER OF THE CORRECT ANSWER IN THE SPACE AT THE RIGHT.*

1. What type of map projection is designed to show all great circle arcs as straight lines for all directions from one or two points?   1.____

    A. Azimuthal   B. Orthogonal
    C. Conformal   D. Standard

2. On maps using plane reference systems, a false origin is sometimes created in order to   2.____

    A. avoid negative coordinates
    B. adjust for overlapping neat lines in a series
    C. close the gaps created by neat lines that do not meet in series
    D. maintain a standard graticule

3. In cartographic applications, a tool known as a(n) _____ is used to trace a curved line through plotted points.   3.____

    A. rose   B. spline   C. scribe   D. compass

4. _____ contours are used by the USGS as single lines representing several contour lines as would occur in portraying vertical or near-vertical features.   4.____

    A. Depression   B. Index
    C. Carrying   D. Intermediate

5. What is the MOST descriptively efficient system of scaling cartographic variables?   5.____

    A. Interval   B. Ordinal   C. Ratio   D. Nominal

6. In aerial photography, the apparent change in position of an object caused by a change in the point of observation is known as   6.____

    A. parallax   B. superimposition
    C. drift   D. nadir

7. In surveying, the procedure known as _____ involves locating an unknown point on a plane through the construction of two angles at two points measured from the straight line joining them.   7.____

    A. bearing and distance   B. resection
    C. norming   D. intersection

8. When drawing on smooth, calendered tracing papers, what grade of black lead pencil should be used?   8.____

    A. 6H-5H   B. 4H-3H   C. 2H-H   D. HB-B

9. On a map surface, one mile is represented by 3.17 inches. What is the scale of the map?   9.____

    A. 1:5,000   B. 1:10,000   C. 1:20,000   D. 1:31,000

71

10. The determination of the important characteristics of cartographic data, the elimination of unwanted detail, and the retention and possible exaggeration of the important characteristics are processes in cartographic generalization broadly defined as

    A. symbolization
    B. classification
    C. simplification
    D. induction

10.____

11. The graphic symbol shown at the right is used by cartographers and other personnel as a signal for the type of drawing to be used during the process of compiling a map. What specification does it indicate?

    A. Mask making
    B. Pen and ink
    C. Drawing
    D. Scribing

11.____

12. For correcting image displacements introduced by the tilt of an aerial photograph, which of the following methods has proved quickest and most convenient?

    A. Graphical techniques
    B. Mathematical transformations
    C. Mechanical methods of reprojection
    D. Optical transformations

12.____

13. The richness of a particular color is described in terms of

    A. value   B. chroma   C. hue   D. tint

13.____

14. A cartographer uses line symbols to portray a statistical surface. If the statistical surface is intersected by parallel planes that are also parallel to the datum, and the intersection lines are orthogonally projected onto one of the planes, a series of _____ results.

    A. isarithmic lines
    B. profiles
    C. hachures
    D. oblique traces

14.____

15. Which of the following is a DISADVANTAGE associated with multilens aerial photography?

    A. A smaller image format than ordinary photography
    B. They involve greater variations in illumination
    C. Its use is limited to a single wave band
    D. The exposures are not made simultaneously

15.____

16. In aerial photography, the normal angle involves a focal length of approximately _____ mm.

    A. 88   B. 152   C. 300   D. 476

16.____

17. Which of the following is NOT a common use for line symbols in mapping?

    A. The assumption of a statistical surface (ratio-scaled volume) and its portrayal by line symbols
    B. Portrayal of flows by varying sizes of lines and secondarily employing differences in value or spacing
    C. Portrayal of existing volumetric data sets as areal data
    D. Nominal portrayal, using primarily variations in the shape of the line symbols, and also hue, if color is available

17.____

18. What is the term for the network of lines shown on the body of a map, sometimes by subdivision of the border?

    A. Grid
    B. Graticule
    C. Scale
    D. Neat lines

19. In computer cartography, what data structure would MOST likely be used to show a lake on a map?

    A. Ring B. Arc C. String D. Stack

20. The most significant graphic component in cartography is generally considered to be

    A. visual contrast
    B. hierarchical organization
    C. visual balance
    D. the figure-ground phenomenon

21. Each of the following is an important element involved in choroplethic mapping EXCEPT the

    A. number of classes
    B. grading of point symbols
    C. size and shape of unit areas
    D. method of class limit determination

22. A rule of thumb for cartographers who wish to achieve high accuracy in plotting is to _____ when measuring and plotting lines.

    A. interpolate
    B. induce
    C. estimate
    D. extrapolate

23. A cartographer is developing a relief map with a scale of 1:5000. If the cartographer uses hachures to depict slopes, the maximum width of the hachures should be _____ mm.

    A. 0.5 to 0.3
    B. 0.4 to 0.2
    C. 0.3 to 0.2
    D. 0.2 to 0.1

24. When symbolizing with dot tint screens, a map maker should generally do each of the following EXCEPT

    A. use very low and very high percentage screens only if absolutely necessary
    B. combine patterns with smooth tones if there is any possibility of the tones being difficult to distinguish from one another
    C. use as many classes as possible
    D. space the tones as far apart on the perceived blackness scale as is consistent with the data

25. In monochrome printing of maps, up to _____ tint screens can be printed on one area.

    A. 2 B. 3 C. 5 D. 8

KEY (CORRECT ANSWERS)

1.	A	11.	D
2.	A	12.	D
3.	B	13.	B
4.	C	14.	A
5.	D	15.	A
6.	A	16.	C
7.	D	17.	C
8.	D	18.	B
9.	C	19.	A
10.	C	20.	A

21. B
22. A
23. B
24. C
25. B

EXAMINATION SECTION
TEST 1

DIRECTIONS: Each question or incomplete statement is followed by several suggested answers or completions. Select the one that BEST answers the question or completes the statement. *PRINT THE LETTER OF THE CORRECT ANSWER IN THE SPACE AT THE RIGHT.*

1. The scale of one inch equals one hundred feet is equivalent to the fraction

    A. 1/100   B. 100/1   C. 1200/1   D. 1/1200

2. The predominant type of imaging used for civil engineering applications is the traditional _____ centimeter format frame aerial photograph.

    A. 19 x 19   B. 21 x 21   C. 23 x 23   D. 25 x 25

3. Both photogrammetry and remote sensing in the past relied on photographs that are

    A. silver borate emulsion products
    B. silver halide emulsion products
    C. ammonium cyanide emulsion products
    D. silver chlorate emulsion products

4. $5 \mu m$ is equal to five _____ of a meter.

    A. ten thousandth   B. hundred thousandth
    C. millionth   D. ten millionth

5. Raw aerial photographs should not be used as a map because of image tilt and

    A. inability to determine the scale of the map with sufficient accuracy
    B. blurred images
    C. parallax
    D. terrain relief

6. If f is the focal length of an aerial camera and H is the height of the airplane above the ground, the scale of the photograph is equal to

    A. f/H+f   B. f/H-f   C. f/H   D. H-f/H+f

7. Of the following statements related to the shape of the earth, the one that is CORRECT is:

    A. A plane through the poles will intersect the surface of the earth in a circle while a plane through the equator will intersect the earth in an ellipse.
    B. A plane through the poles will intersect the surface of the earth in an ellipse while a plane through the equator will intersect the surface of the earth in a circle.
    C. A plane through the poles will intersect the surface of the earth in a circle while a plane through the equator will intersect the surface of the earth in a circle.
    D. A plane through the poles will intersect the surface of the earth in an ellipse while a plane through the equator will intersect the surface of the earth in an ellipse.

8. The latitude of New York City is MOST NEARLY

   A. 36°-45'N   B. 38°-45'N   C. 40°-45'N   D. 42°-45'N

9. The azimuth of a line is its direction as given by the angle between the meridian and the line measured in a

   A. clockwise direction usually from the south branch of the meridian
   B. counterclockwise direction usually from the south branch of the meridian
   C. clockwise direction usually from the north branch of the meridian
   D. counterclockwise direction usually from the north branch of the meridian

10. A geometric map projection in which the projection surface is a plane tangent to the sphere at any point and the point used as a projection center is the center of the sphere is a(n) _____ projection.

    A. stereographic   B. gnomonic
    C. orthographic   D. equal area

11. A map projection showing the correct angle between any pair of intersecting lines making small areas that seems to have a correct shape is known as _____ projection.

    A. conformal   B. isoclinic
    C. isometric   D. axonometric

12. The projection on which circles on the earth will appear as circles on the map is a(n) _____ projection.

    A. isometric   B. orthographic
    C. gnomonic   D. stereographic

13. An orthographic projection whose projection surface is a plane tangent to the sphere has its projection center at

    A. the center of the sphere
    B. the end of the diameter opposite to the point of tangency
    C. an infinite distance from the plane
    D. a variable distance from the plane

14. The *disadvantage* of the Mercator projection is that

    A. a line of constant bearing is a straight line on the map
    B. areas are distorted in size
    C. the scale at the equator is never accurate
    D. the meridians are not parallel on the map

15. An advantage of geographic coordinates is that it

    A. is more accurate than any other system
    B. is easier to determine than any other system
    C. has universal recognition
    D. can be determined by astronomical surveying

16. The conic projection with two standard parallels is known as the _____ conformal projector. 16.____

    A. Mercator   B. Albers
    C. Transverse Mercator   D. Lambert

17. The conic projection with two standard parallels is used for the plane coordinate system for states 17.____

    A. having conical shapes
    B. that are nearly square shaped
    C. that have greater north-south than east-west extent
    D. that have greater east-west than north-south extent

18. The Mercator projection is a projection on a cylinder that is frequently tangent to the earth at 18.____

    A. zero degrees longitude   B. 90 degrees longitude
    C. 90 degrees latitude   D. the equator

19. The Transverse Mercator Projection is used for the state plane coordinate system for states 19.____

    A. having conical shapes
    B. that are nearly square shaped
    C. that have greater north-south than east-west extent
    D. that have greater east-west than north-south extent

20. A vertical aerial photograph usually cannot be used as a map primarily because of 20.____

    A. blurred image and terrain relief
    B. improper focal length and improper height
    C. blurred image and incorrect height
    D. terrain relief and image tilt

21. Of the following statements relating to aerial photographs, the CORRECT answer is the 21.____

    A. smaller the scale, the smaller the area covered
    B. higher the altitude of the plane, the larger the scale of the photograph
    C. area covered by a fixed size photograph varies inversely as the square of the scale
    D. focal length of the camera is not a determining factor in the scale of the photograph

22. Rectification of an aerial photograph 22.____

    A. corrects for the ground not being flat
    B. eliminates error due to the airplane not being at the correct height when the photograph is taken
    C. corrects for error in the overlap of the photographs
    D. corrects for error due to the axis of the camera not being vertical when the shot was taken

23. An aerial photograph with distortions removed is termed a(n) 23.____

    A. isophoto   B. planophoto
    C. orthophoto   D. rectophoto

24. Viewing an object with one eye closed and then the other eye closed reveals a displacement of the object.
    This is known as

    A. double vision
    B. apparent displacement
    C. visual distortion
    D. parallax

25. A panchromatic emulsion used in aerial photography is

    A. red and white only
    B. blue, red and white
    C. black and white
    D. black, red, blue and white

KEY (CORRECT ANSWERS)

1. D	11. A
2. C	12. D
3. B	13. C
4. C	14. B
5. D	15. C
6. C	16. D
7. B	17. D
8. C	18. D
9. C	19. C
10. B	20. D

21. C
22. D
23. C
24. D
25. C

TEST 2

DIRECTIONS: Each question or incomplete statement is followed by several suggested answers or completions. Select the one that BEST answers the question or completes the statement. *PRINT THE LETTER OF THE CORRECT ANSWER IN THE SPACE AT THE RIGHT.*

1. In the diagram shown at the right, h equals

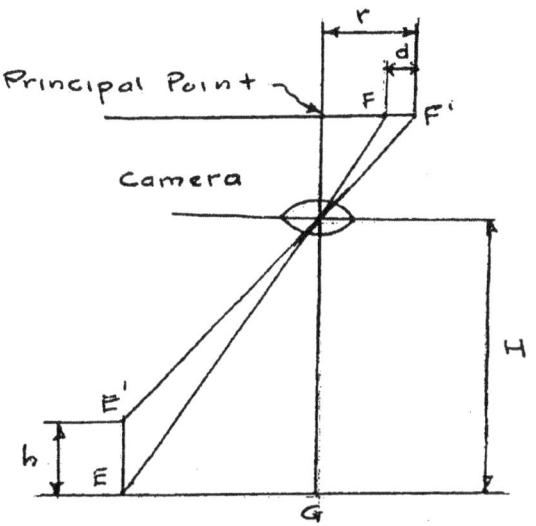

   A. dH/r
   B. rH/d
   C. dr/H
   D. H/dr

   1.____

2. In the diagram for the previous problem, G is the

   A. nadir point B. low point
   C. zenith point D. ground zero

   2.____

3. The focal length for a camera is 145 mm. Its focal length, in inches, is MOST NEARLY

   A. 5.65 B. 5.68 C. 5.71 D. 5.74

   3.____

4. The MOST common size lens used in aerial photogrammetric mapping is

   A. 3.5" B. 6" C. 8.25" D. 12"

   4.____

5. A satellite used in acquiring land imagery from space is

   A. Telstar B. Spot C. Minos D. Tiros

   5.____

6. The sensors used on a satellite are usually

   A. mechanical-optical B. electro-mechanical
   C. film based D. electro-optical

   6.____

7. A single detector on a satellite imager is a

   A. spacial resolution B. spot
   C. photomultiplier D. pixel

   7.____

8. The scanner on a satellite imager scans

   A. across track
   B. parallel to the track
   C. first across track and then parallel to track
   D. first parallel to track and then across track

9. The Landsats 4 and 5 MSS have _____ bands.

   A. 5   B. 6   C. 7   D. 8

10. MSS is an abbreviation for

    A. multispectral scanner
    B. multisized spacers
    C. mechanical spectral scanner
    D. multispectral system

11. CCD is the abbreviation for

    A. charge-coupled devices
    B. charged capacitance detectors
    C. close-range couple detectors
    D. close-range charged devices

12. Of the following, the one that is a scanning mode is _____ sensors.

    A. linear array   B. image swath
    C. push-broom linear   D. close-range linear

13. A vertical aerial photograph was taken from a plane flying at an altitude of 5000 meters. The ground elevation is 276 meters. The focal length is 152.4 mm. The scale of the photograph is MOST NEARLY

    A. 1/31000   B. 1/32000   C. 1/33000   D. 1/34000

14. The effect of relief on the location of image points is known as

    A. relief tilt   B. relief effect
    C. parallax   D. relief displacement

15. The area in square inches of a 20 centimeters by 20 centimeters square is MOST NEARLY

    A. 62   B. 64   C. 66   D. 68

16. Some mosaics made from aerial photographs are quite inexact in scale, especially when

    A. there are grade crossing overpasses on the map
    B. there is considerable change in elevation on the ground
    C. a tall building appears on the mosaic
    D. the elevation of the plane changes while the photographs are taken

17. In aerial photography there is a film shift in the direction of flight during exposure whose purpose is to

    A. correct for timing inconsistency
    B. compensate for tilt
    C. minimize image blur
    D. compensate for drift

17.____

18. The intervalometer is set to insure the

    A. correct v/H
    B. correct amount of light enters the camera
    C. proper size of photographs
    D. proper overlap of adjacent photographs

18.____

19. CAD is an abbreviation for

    A. computer analog drafting
    B. calculation assisted drafting
    C. computer-aided design
    D. calculation assisted design

19.____

20. The analysis of aerial photographs and images for the purpose of extracting the best interpretation of the image content is the definition of

    A. quantitative photographic interpretation
    B. high resolution photography
    C. remote sensing
    D. image reflection

20.____

21. The number of degrees longitude the sun moves in one hour is

    A. 5   B. 10   C. 15   D. 20

21.____

22. The ecliptic is the projection on the surface of the earth of

    A. an asteroid   B. the North Star
    C. the moon   D. the sun

22.____

23. The plane of the earth's orbit around the sun is termed the orbit plane. The number of degrees that an axis perpendicular to the orbit plane goes through the center of the earth with the axis of the earth is MOST NEARLY

    A. 21 1/2   B. 23 1/2   C. 25 1/2   D. 27 1/2

23.____

24. Looking from above, the direction the sun moves about the earth in a year and the rotation of the earth about its axis is in a

    A. counterclockwise direction and the earth rotates about its axis in a counterclockwise direction
    B. counterclockwise direction and the earth rotates about its axis in a clockwise direction
    C. clockwise direction and the earth rotates about its axis in a counterclockwise direction
    D. clockwise direction and the earth rotates about its axis in a clockwise direction

24.____

25. A solstice can occur on

　　A. March 21
　　B. December 22
　　C. January 1
　　D. June 21

KEY (CORRECT ANSWERS)

1. A
2. A
3. C
4. B
5. B

6. D
7. D
8. A
9. C
10. A

11. A
12. C
13. A
14. D
15. A

16. B
17. C
18. D
19. C
20. C

21. C
22. D
23. B
24. C
25. D

TEST 3

DIRECTIONS: Each question or incomplete statement is followed by several suggested answers or completions. Select the one that BEST answers the question or completes the statement. *PRINT THE LETTER OF THE CORRECT ANSWER IN THE SPACE AT THE RIGHT.*

1. Metrology is the study of
   A. the earth's composition
   B. the earth's surface
   C. comets and meteors
   D. weights and measures

2. The intersection of a tilted aerial photograph and a vertical photograph is an
   A. axis of inclination
   B. isocline
   C. isoline
   D. isocenter

3. In a vertical aerial photograph with varying relief, the higher the relief the
   A. higher the scale and the higher the displacement
   B. higher the scale and the lower the displacement
   C. lower the relief and the higher the displacement
   D. lower the relief and the lower the displacement

4. An instrument used to produce a photograph in which the tilt has been eliminated is a(n)
   A. orthophotographer
   B. rectifier
   C. stereoplotter
   D. monocomparator

5. The instrument composed of a two-axis stage with a measuring microscope and coordinate readout is a
   A. stereoplotter
   B. monocomparator
   C. analytic plotter
   D. rectifier

6. Softcopy as a restitution system is
   A. optical
   B. mechanical
   C. digital
   D. analytical

7. 20°-18'-30" is, in decimals of a degree, MOST NEARLY
   A. 20.2783   B. 20.2883   C. 20.2983   D. 20.3083

8. 21.5384° is, in degrees, minutes and seconds, MOST NEARLY
   A. 21°-32'-18.24"
   B. 21°-32'-5.12"
   C. 21°-31'-52.16"
   D. 21°-31'-23.18"

9. The angle between the true meridian and the magnetic meridian is the magnetic
   A. dip
   B. declination
   C. inclination
   D. offset

10. The method surveyors usually use in determining elevations on a construction job is _____ levelling.

    A. differential
    B. stadia
    C. reciprocal
    D. trigonometric

11. One radian is, in degrees, MOST NEARLY

    A. 57.2758   B. 57.2958   C. 57.3158   D. 57.3358

12. A planimeter is used to measure

    A. dip   B. strike   C. area   D. volume

13. Assume a circle has 400 degrees instead of the usual 360 degrees. Seventy-five degrees would be, on a 400 degree circle, MOST NEARLY in degrees

    A. 83.167   B. 83.25   C. 83.283   D. 83.333

14. The unit measurement of area in the metric system is the

    A. tesla   B. pascal   C. hectare   D. farad

15. One meter is, in inches, MOST NEARLY

    A. 39.37   B. 39.27   C. 39.17   D. 39.07

16. One inch, in centimeters, is

    A. 2.44   B. 2.54   C. 2.64   D. 2.34

17. A nautical mile is, in feet,

    A. 5966   B. 6000   C. 6046   D. 6076

18. One kilometer, in miles, is

    A. .57   B. .62   C. .67   D. .72

19. A chain is equal to _____ feet.

    A. 66   B. 68   C. 70   D. 72

20. The number of square feet in an acre is

    A. 43470   B. 43560   C. 43650   D. 43740

21. The number that must be added to $x^2 + 8x$ to complete the square is

    A. 16   B. 32   C. 48   D. 64

22. The area of an equilateral whose side is 9 is

    A. $\frac{49}{4}\sqrt{3}$ B. $\frac{16\sqrt{3}}{3}$ C. $\frac{81\sqrt{3}}{4}$ D. $27\sqrt{3}$

23. In the United States, the length or width of a normal township is _____ miles.

    A. 5   B. 6   C. 7   D. 8

24. A row of townships extending north and south is called a 24.____
    A. guide   B. vertical   C. tier   D. range

25. The area of a township, in square miles, is 25.____
    A. 25   B. 36   C. 49   D. 64

KEY (CORRECT ANSWERS)

1. D
2. C
3. A
4. B
5. B

6. C
7. D
8. A
9. B
10. A

11. B
12. C
13. D
14. C
15. A

16. B
17. D
18. B
19. A
20. B

21. A
22. C
23. B
24. D
25. B

TEST 4

DIRECTIONS: Each question or incomplete statement is followed by several suggested answers or completions. Select the one that BEST answers the question or completes the statement. *PRINT THE LETTER OF THE CORRECT ANSWER IN THE SPACE AT THE RIGHT.*

1. The right of the people or government to take private property for public use upon payment of just compensation is the definition of

    A. easement
    B. eminent domain
    C. encroachment
    D. escheat

    1._____

2. An absolute or ownership in property including unlimited power of alienation is the definition of

    A. fee simple
    B. guarantee title
    C. general warrantee deed
    D. escheat

    2._____

3. Within a deed is a designation of natural objects, monuments, course, distance or other matters of description as limits of the boundaries is the definition of

    A. appurtenances
    B. abstract of title
    C. metes and bounds description
    D. call

    3._____

Questions 4-5.

DIRECTIONS: Questions 4 and 5 refer to the statement below.

"If you wish to sail from one port to another," a map maker wrote in the sixteenth century, "here is a chart, and a straight line on it, and if you follow this line carefully you will certainly arrive at your destination. But the length of the line may not be correct."

4. This line is called a(n) _____ line.

    A. azimuth
    B. true
    C. rhumb
    D. great circle

    4._____

5. The projection used is usually a(n) _____ projection.

    A. albers   B. conic   C. Mercator   D. Lambert

    5._____

6. Topographic maps in the United States are made according to the _____ projection.

    A. Mercator
    B. polyconic
    C. cylindrical central
    D. cylindrical equal spaced

    6._____

7. On a map the bearing of line EF is N18° E and the bearing of line EG is S67° W. Angle FEG is equal to, in degrees,

    A. 131   B. 175   C. 85   D. 229

    7._____

8. The radius of a circle in which a central angle of one degree subtends an arc of 100 feet is MOST NEARLY _____ feet.

   A. 5700   B. 5730   C. 5760   D. 5790

9. A magnetic azimuth of 54°-00' was observed along line EF in January 2000. The declination for the area is found from an isogonic chart dated 1990 to be 15°-30'E with an annual change of 2' westward. The true azimuth of line EF is

   A. 39°-10'E   B. 39°-30'E   C. 69°-10'E   D. 69°-50'E

10. If the scale on a map is 1:50000, a mile would be _____ inches.

    A. 1.21   B. 1.23   C. 1.25   D. 1.27

11. On a map there may be three norths: true north, magnetic north and _____ north.

    A. geodetic   B. geographic
    C. grid   D. mercator

12. In taping with a 100 foot steel tape, one end of the tape is one foot higher than the other end of the tape. This will introduce an error in measuring, in inches, MOST NEARLY

    A. 1/64   B. 1/32   C. 1/16   D. 1/8

13. $\sin(x+90°)$ is equal to

    A. $\sin x$ B. $\cos x$ C. $-\sin x$ D. $-\cos x$

14. $\cos^2 x - \sin^2 x$ is equal to

    A. $\sin 2x$ B. $-\sin 2x$ C. $\cos 2x$ D. $-\cos 2x$

15. The quadrant in which sin x and cos x are negative is

    A. I   B. II   C. III   D. IV

16. EDM is an abbreviation for electronic _____ measurement.

    A. direct   B. decimal   C. distance   D. data

17. In surveying with a level, a point used in the leveling process to temporarily transfer the elevation from one setup to the next is a

    A. PI   B. TP   C. FS   D. ES

18. Positional and navigational data from the GPS are provided to the community through PPS or SPS.
    SPS is the abbreviation for

    A. Selective Positioning System
    B. Stationary Positioning System
    C. Standard Positioning Service
    D. Standard Positioning System

19. The pattern of illuminated horizontal scanning lines formed on a television picture tube when no signal is being received is

    A. static   B. parallax   C. raster   D. overlap

20. Project planning starts with the maps to be produced. The restraints on the choices available to the planner are

    A. area to be covered and the cost of the end product
    B. accuracy of the maps and the cost of the maps
    C. use of airplanes or satellites and the precision of the maps
    D. the detailed information the map is to supply and the area to be covered

21. The technical name for the North Star is

    A. Arcturus   B. Andromeda
    C. Polaris   D. Vega

22. The constellation in which the North Star appears is

    A. Virgo   B. Cassiopeia
    C. Ursa Major   D. Ursa Minor

23. A right cone is cut by a plane perpendicular to the base of the cone. The curve formed by the intersection of the surface of the cone and the plane is a

    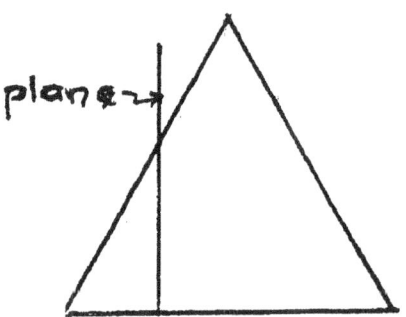

    A. hyperbola
    B. parabola
    C. half of an ellipse
    D. none of the above

24. A topographic map has a scale of one inch equals 40 feet. The contours are every 5 feet. The horizontal distance between two adjacent contours is 3/4 inch. The slope of the earth at that line is, in degrees, MOST NEARLY

    A. 9 1/2   B. 11 1/2   C. 13 1/2   D. 15 1/2

25. $\sin \frac{x}{2}$ is equal to

    A. $\dfrac{\sqrt{1+\cos x}}{2}$ B. $\dfrac{\sqrt{1-\cos x}}{2}$ C. $\sqrt{\dfrac{1+\cos x}{2}}$ D. $\sqrt{\dfrac{1-\cos x}{2}}$

KEY (CORRECT ANSWERS)

1.	B	11.	C
2.	A	12.	C
3.	D	13.	B
4.	C	14.	C
5.	C	15.	C
6.	B	16.	C
7.	A	17.	B
8.	B	18.	C
9.	C	19.	C
10.	D	20.	B

21. C
22. D
23. A
24. A
25. B

EXAMINATION SECTION
TEST 1

DIRECTIONS: Each question or incomplete statement is followed by several suggested answers or completions. Select the one that BEST answers the question or completes the statement. *PRINT THE LETTER OF THE CORRECT ANSWER IN THE SPACE AT THE RIGHT.*

1. If a map has a scale of 1" = 1 mile, a fractional equivalent would be

    A. $\dfrac{1}{63360}$ B. $\dfrac{1}{5280}$ C. $\dfrac{1}{1000}$ D. $\dfrac{1}{1200}$

    1.____

2. The diameter of the earth is MOST NEARLY _____ miles.

    A. 5,000 B. 6,000 C. 7,000 D. 8,000

    2.____

3. An instrument used to reproduce a drawing at a different scale is called a

    A. psychrometer B. manometer
    C. planimeter   D. pantograph

    3.____

4. A baseline is measured many times and the length was found to be 594.32 ± .01'. This reading means

    A. none of the measurements was less than 594.31' nor more than 594.33'
    B. 594.32' is not the accepted measurement of the length
    C. ±.01 is a measure of the accuracy of 594.32'
    D. 594.32' is two standard deviations from 594.32'

    4.____

5. The engineering societies have accepted the metric system for use in engineering design. This was done despite the fact that

    A. the metric system is easy to use
    B. it will be easy to switch from the current system
    C. it is easy for tradesmen to build based on metric measurements
    D. the United States remains one of the few countries not using the metric system

    5.____

6. One radian is MOST NEARLY _____ degrees.

    A. 56.3 B. 57.3 C. 58.3 D. 59.3

    6.____

7. Of the following statements relating to the hkrdhess of pencil leads, the one that is CORRECT is

    A. B is harder than H   B. HB is harder than H
    C. F is harder than HB   D. B is harder than HB

    7.____

8. A 24" x 36" drafting paper has a 1/2 inch boundary. To check that the rectangle is not skewed, the BEST method is to

    A. check that the rectangle is exactly 1/2 inch from the edge of the paper
    B. check that the diagonals of the rectangle are equal in measure
    C. measure the opposite sides of the rectangle to insure they are equal
    D. use a T-square and triangles to insure the opposite sides are parallel

    8.____

9. Using a 30°-60°-90° right triangle and a 45 right triangle, it is relatively easy to draw an angle of _____ degrees.

   A. 15 B. 25 C. 35 D. 55

10. The angle that the needle on the compass of a transit makes with the true meridian is termed the _____ of the needle.

   A. inclination B. variation
   C. offset D. declination

11. The _____ line contains the points of zero magnetic deviation from true North.

   A. zero dip B. secular variation
   C. true magnetic bearing D. agonic

12. The contour map of a hill is shown at the right. The shape of the hill is MOST NEARLY a(n)

   A. cone
   B. hemisphere
   C. paraboloid
   D. ellipsoid

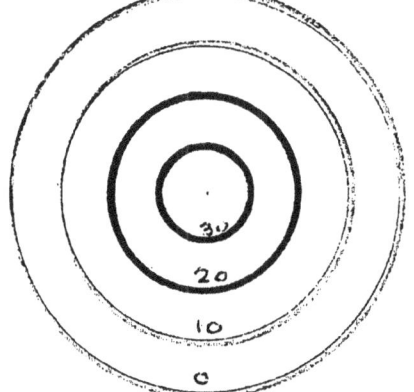

13. The contour map of a hemisphere would appear as in

A.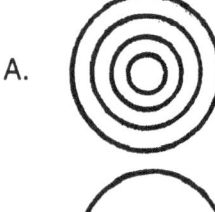

B.

C.

D.

14. [diagram: Contour Crossing A Street — sidewalk, down grade, roadway, sidewalk]

    Contour Crossing
    A Street

    Of the following, the contour that is CORRECT is

    A. [diagram]   B. [diagram]
    C. [diagram]   D. [diagram]

15. *An outstanding claim or encumbrance which if valid will affect or impair the owner's title* defines

    A. condemnation
    B. demise
    C. consequential damage
    D. cloud of title

16. *The body of principles developed from immemorial usage and custom which receive judicial recognition and sanction through repeated application* is the definition of _____ law.

    A. legislated
    B. de facto
    C. common
    D. historic

17. *An absolute estate or ownership in property including unlimited power of alienation* is the definition of

    A. guarantee title
    B. fee simple
    C. general warranty deed
    D. grantee

18. ——x——x——x on a map represents a(n)

    A. discontinued road
    B. overhead power line
    C. hedge
    D. fence

19. —+—+—+—+—+— on a map represents a

    A. discontinued road
    B. property line that was eliminated
    C. railroad
    D. power line

20. One acre is equal to _____ square feet.

    A. 42,650   B. 42,560   C. 43,650   D. 43,560

21. Liber is a

    A. map B. deed C. plan D. book

22. Riparian rights are rights to

    A. minerals under the land
    B. sinking wells to draw water from the aquafer
    C. gain access to their property
    D. of waterfront land in the use of the bed and banks of the water

23. A rod is equal to _____ yards.

    A. 4 1/2 B. 5 C. 5 1/2 D. 6

24. A planimeter is used to measure

    A. area
    B. angles
    C. bearings
    D. the length of lines

25. A chain is a unit of land measurement equal to _____ feet.

    A. 60 B. 62 C. 64 D. 66

KEY (CORRECT ANSWERS)

1. A
2. D
3. D
4. C
5. D

6. B
7. C
8. B
9. A
10. D

11. D
12. A
13. B
14. D
15. D

16. C
17. B
18. D
19. C
20. D

21. D
22. D
23. C
24. A
25. D

TEST 2

DIRECTIONS: Each question or incomplete statement is followed by several suggested answers or completions. Select the one that BEST answers the question or completes the statement. *PRINT THE LETTER OF THE CORRECT ANSWER IN THE SPACE AT THE RIGHT.*

1. Eminent domain is defined as 1.____

    A. the government's position prevailing in a dispute with an individual
    B. the original ownership of property in the government
    C. an instrument in writing by which property is transferred from a private party to the government
    D. the right of government to take private property for public use upon payment of just compensation

2. 32°-20"-30" is equal to 2.____

    A. 32.3417   B. 32.3503   C. 32.3587   D. 32.3617

3. 34.5120 degrees is equal to 3.____

    A. 34°-30'-43.2"   B. 34°-30'-53.2"
    C. 34°-31'-03.2"   D. 34°-31'-13.2"

4. .01 feet is MOST NEARLY _____ inch(es). 4.____

    A. 1/8   B. 5/32   C. 3/16   D. 7/32

5. One inch is equal to _____ centimeters. 5.____

    A. 2.44   B. 2.54   C. 2.64   D. 2.74

Questions 6-8

DIRECTIONS: Questions 6 to 8, inclusive, refer to the field notes for a quadrilateral ABCD.

Line	Length	Bearing
AB	50.00	N30°-00'E
BC	80.00	S60°-00'E
CD	130.00	S30°-00'N
DA		

6. The area of the quadrilateral is equal to _____ square feet. 6.____

    A. 7,000   B. 7,200   C. 7,400   D. 7,600

7. The bearing of line DA is 7.____

    A. N10°-00'W   B. N15°-00'W   C. N20°-00'W   D. N30°-00'W

8. The length of DA is _____ feet. 8.____

    A. 113.14   B. 115.14   C. 117.14   D. 119.14

9. Of the following, the instrument MOST closely related to a transit is a

    A. level
    B. plane table
    C. sextant
    D. theodolite

10. Azimuth is usually measured _____ from the _____.

    A. clockwise; south
    B. counterclockwise; south
    C. clockwise; north
    D. counterclockwise; north

11. The usual length of a steel surveying tape is _____ feet.

    A. 50
    B. 75
    C. 100
    D. 200

12. The number of yards in a mile is

    A. 1,740
    B. 1,750
    C. 1,760
    D. 1,770

13. The scale of a drawing is one inch equals one foot. The scale ratio of the drawing is

    A. 1/12
    B. 1/144
    C. 1/48
    D. 1/192

14. 0° longitude goes through the city of

    A. Greenwich, England
    B. London, England
    C. Paris, France
    D. Versailles, France

15. A _____ map shows the configuration of the terrain and location of natural and man-made objects.

    A. geographic
    B. hydrographic
    C. geodetic
    D. topographic

16. The geometric shape of the earth is MOST NEARLY a(n)

    A. part of a paraboloid
    B. sphere
    C. ellipsoid
    D. part of a hyperboloid

17. New York City is at latitude

    A. 35° N
    B. 40° N
    C. 45° N
    D. 50° N

18. New York City is at longitude

    A. 62° W
    B. 66° W
    C. 70° W
    D. 74° W

19. The Mercator projection is frequently used for maps in high school textbooks. The disadvantage in using Mercator projection is that

    A. directions are distorted
    B. the greatest distortion is at the equator
    C. longitudes are inaccurate
    D. areas are distorted

20. The MOST commonly used projection in the world for engineering work is the _____ projection.

    A. Mercator
    B. Albers conformal
    C. Lambert conformal conic
    D. Thales

Questions 21-25.

DIRECTIONS: Questions 21 through 25, inclusive, refer to the diagram below.

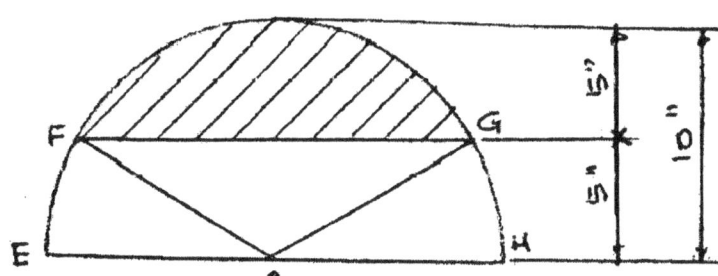

21. The area of the semicircle is MOST NEARLY _____ square inches.   21.____
    A. 151   B. 153   C. 155   D. 157

22. The area of triangle FOG is MOST NEARLY _____ square inches.   22.____
    A. 41.3   B. 43.3   C. 45.3   D. 47.3

23. Angle EOF is _____ degrees.   23.____
    A. 20   B. 25   C. 30   D. 35

24. The area of the sector EOF is _____ square inches.   24.____
    A. 26.2   B. 28.2   C. 30.2   D. 32.2

25. The shaded area is, in square inches, MOST NEARLY   25.____
    A. 55.3   B. 57.3   C. 49.3   D. 61.3

KEY (CORRECT ANSWERS)

1. D
2. A
3. A
4. A
5. B

6. B
7. B
8. A
9. D
10. C

11. C
12. C
13. A
14. A
15. D

16. C
17. B
18. D
19. D
20. C

21. D
22. B
23. C
24. A
25. D

EXAMINATION SECTION

TEST 1

DIRECTIONS: For each question or statement, write the letter in the space at right that best answers the question or completes the statement.

1. The Mercator map is still widely used
   A. for geodetic surveying
   B. in navigation
   C. when areas under consideration are small
   D. where the distance between points on the map are important

   1._____

2. The number of radians in a semicircle is
   A. $\pi/2$ B. $3/4\,\pi$ C. π D. $3/2\,\pi$

   2._____

3.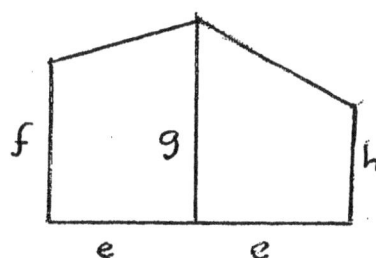

   The formula for the area of the figure shown above is
   A. $\dfrac{e(f+h)}{2} + eg$ B. $\dfrac{e(f+g+h)}{2}$ C. $2e(f+g+h)$ D. $2eg + \dfrac{e(f+h)}{2}$

   3._____

4.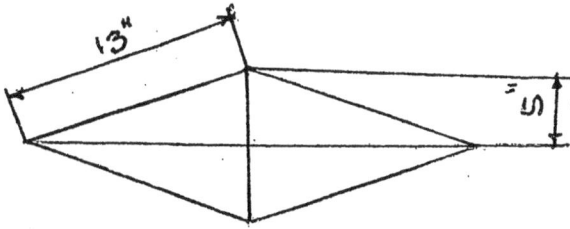

   The area of the rhombus shown above is _____ square inches.
   A. 110   B. 115   C. 120   D. 125

   4._____

5. A(n) _____ is a unit of area in the metric system.
   A. pentare   B. hectare   C. octare   D. sectare

   5._____

6. A kilometer is MOST NEARLY equal to _____ miles.
   A. 0.45   B. 0.5   C. 0.55   D. 0.6

   6._____

7. If the scale of a drawing is 3/16" = 1'-0, a distance of 49 feet would measure on the drawing most nearly _____ inches.
   A. 9   B. 9 3/16   C. 9 3/8   D. 9 1/2

7._____

8. The area of an equilateral triangle of side 10 is most nearly
   A. 43.3   B. 44.3   C. 45.3   D. 46.3

8._____

9. The interior angle of a regular pentagon is equal to _____ degrees.
   A. 106   B. 108   C. 110   D. 112

9._____

10. The area of a regular octagon inscribed in a circle of radius 10" is MOST NEARLY _____ square inches.
    A. 283   B. 280   C. 277   D. 274

10._____

11.

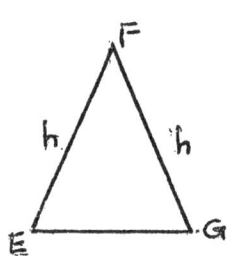

The area of the isosceles triangle is
A. $\dfrac{h^2 \sin E \cos E}{2}$ B. $\dfrac{h^2 \cos 2E}{2}$ C. $\dfrac{h^2 \sin 2E}{2}$ D. $\dfrac{h^2 \sin^2 E}{2}$

11._____

12.

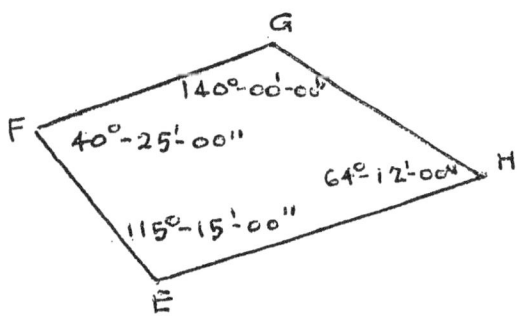

A survey was made of the quadrilateral shown above. The total error in the angular measurements is to be equally divided among the angles. The adjusted value of angle H is
A. 64°-13'-00"   B. 64°-14'-00"   C. 64°-15'-00"   D. 64°-16'-00"

12._____

13. The difference between true North and magnetic North at a given point on the ground is known as the _____ at the point.
    A. dip
    B. inclination
    C. recession
    D. declination

13._____

14.

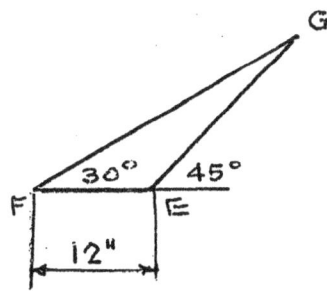

If the area of triangle EFG is 42 square inches, the distance GE is most nearly _____ inches.
A. 9.3   B. 9.5   C. 9.7   D. 9.9

14._____

15. Arc cos √3 is
         2

    A. 30°   B. 45°   C. 60°   D. 75°

15._____

16. Elevation 43.27' is equal to
    A. 43'-3 1/8"   B. 43'-3 3/16"   C. 43'-3 1/4"   D. 43'-3 5/16"

16._____

17. A millimeter is one _____ of a meter.
    A. tenth
    B. hundredth
    C. thousandth
    D. ten thousandth

17._____

18.

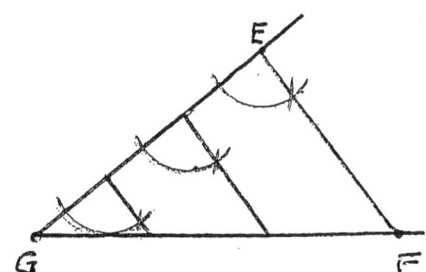

The primary purpose of the geometric construction is to
A. draw similar triangles
B. trisect line EF
C. trisect line Ge
D. trisect line GF

Questions 19 to 21 refer to the data below.

1, 5, 8, 8, 10, 10, 10, 13, 16

19. The mean of the data is
    A. 7 B. 8 C. 9 D. 10

20. The median of the data is
    A. 5 B. 8 C. 10 D. 13

21. The mode of the data is
    A. 8 B. 10 C. 13 D. 16

22.

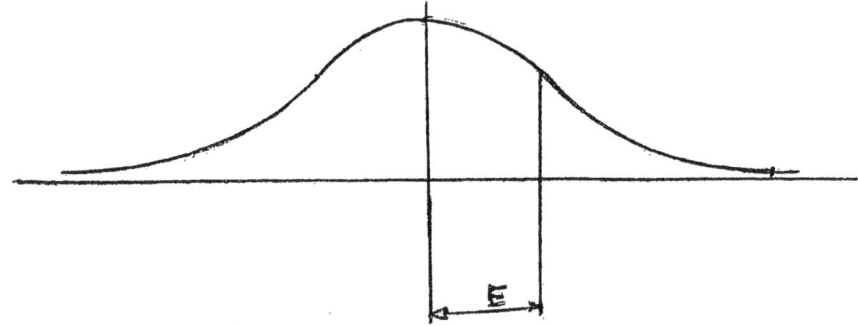

Shown above is a curve showing a normal distribution.
E is one standard deviation and is equal to
A. 30% B. 32% C. 34% D. 36%

23.

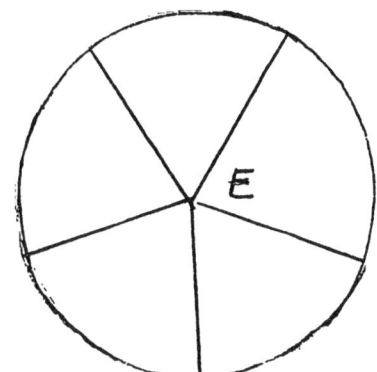

The pie chart shown above represents the distribution of data. If E represents one fifth of the total data, it is equal to
A. 66°　　　B. 68°　　　C. 70°　　　D. 72°

24.

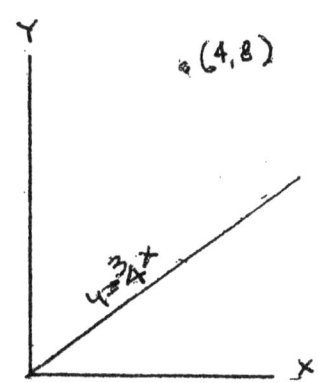

The distance from the point (4,8) to the line y = 3/4 x is MOST NEARLY
A. 3.0　　　B. 3.5　　　C. 4.0　　　D. 4.5

25. $4 \sum_{X=1} X$ is equal to

A. 4　　　B. 10　　　C. 16　　　D. 30

KEY (CORRECT ANSWERS)

1. B
2. C
3. A
4. C
5. B
6. D
7. B
8. A
9. B
10. A

11. C
12. B
13. D
14. D
15. A
16. C
17. C
18. D
19. C
20. C

21. D
22. C
23. D
24. C
25. B

TEST 2

DIRECTIONS: For each question or statement, write the letter in the space at right that best answers the question or completes the statement.

1.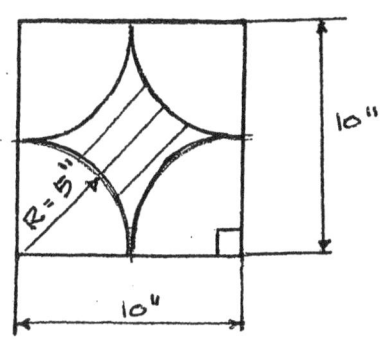

    The shaded area is equal to _____ square inches.
    A. 18.5 B. 19.5 C. 20.5 D. 21.5

    1._____

2.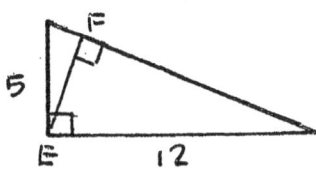

    EF is equal to
    A. 4.42 B. 4.52 C. 4.62 D. 4.72

    2._____

3. $\log_4 64$ is equal to
    A. 2 B. 3 C. 4 D. 5

    3._____

4.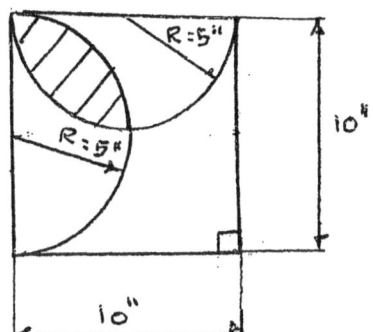

    The shaded area is equal to _____ square inches.
    A. 13.8 B. 14.3 C. 14.8 D. 15.3

    4._____

Questions 5 and 6 refer to a parabola.

5. The low point of the parabola $y = x^2 - 6x$ occurs when x =
   A. 3   B. 4   C. 5   D. 6

   5._____

6. The value of y at the low point on the parabola is
   A. –3   B. –6   C. –9   D. –12

   6._____

---

7. The point inside a scalene triangle that is the intersection of the perpendicular bisector of each side of the triangle
   A. is the center of the circumscribed circle of the triangle.
   B. is the center of the inscribed circle of the triangle.
   C. divides each line in the ratio of one to two
   D. has none of the above properties

   7._____

8.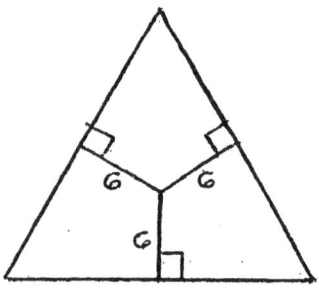

   Shown above is an equilateral triangle. The perimeter of the triangle is
   A. 36√2   B. 36√3   C. 54   D. 72

   8._____

9.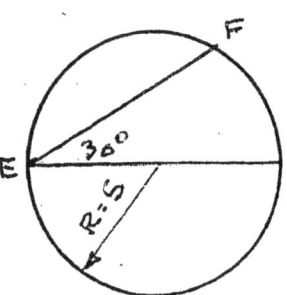

   Chord EF is equal to
   A. 8.1   B. 8.4   C. 8.7   D. 9.0

   9._____

3.(#2)

10.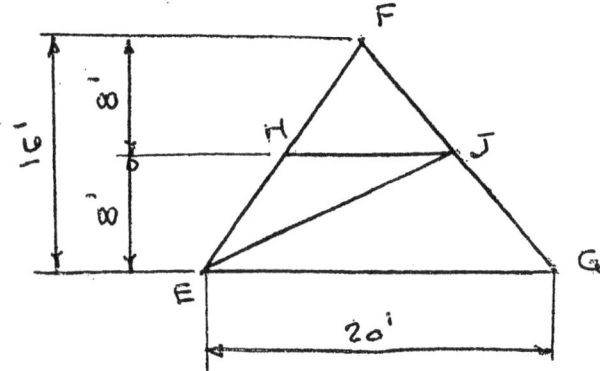

FE = FG
HJ is parallel to EG

EJ is equal to
A. 16.5'   B. 17'   C. 17.5'   D. 18.0'

10._____

11.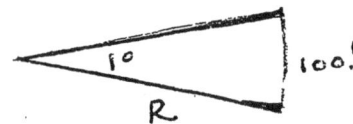

The radius of a circle where a central angle of 1 degree subtends an arc of 100 feet is
A. 5721'   B. 5724'   C. 5727'   D. 5730'

11._____

12.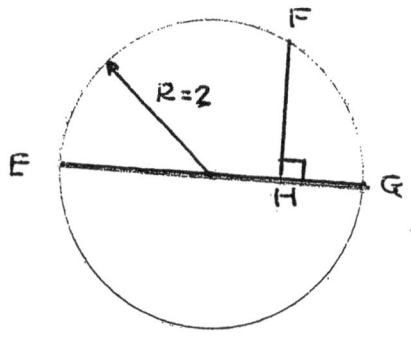

$\overline{EH} = 3$
$\overline{HG} = 1$

FH is equal to
A. $\sqrt{3}$ B. 1.75   C. $\sqrt{2}$ D. 1.5

12._____

13. $\sin \dfrac{x}{2} =$

A. $\dfrac{\sqrt{1+\cos x}}{2}$ B. $\dfrac{\sqrt{1-\cos x}}{2}$ C. $\dfrac{\sqrt{1+\sin x}}{2}$ D. $\dfrac{\sqrt{1-\sin x}}{2}$

13._____

14. Sin (x + y) =
    A. sinx cosy + cosx siny
    B. sinx cosy − cosx siny
    C. cosx cosy + sinx siny
    D. cosx cosy − sinx siny

14._____

15. A fair coin with a head and tail is flipped 3 times. The probability of 3 tails is
    A. 1/4 B. 1/8 C. 1/12 D. 1/16

15._____

16. A vertical bar graph that illustrates a frequency distribution with rectangles erected on a horizontal axis is a
    A. cumulative frequency
    B. scattergram
    C. rectogram
    D. histogram

16._____

17. A student taking a test was told that his mark on the test was in the fifty-fifth percentile. This means that
    A. he received a rating of 55 percent on the test
    B. he received a higher rating than 55 percent of the students
    C. 55 percent of the students passed the test
    D. he was among the 55 percent of the students passing the test

17._____

18. CADD is an abbreviation for Computer Aided
    A. Design and Drafting
    B. Design and Detailing
    C. Drafting and Detailing
    D. none of the above

18._____

19.

19._____

In the rectangle solid, EF is equal to
A. √19   B. √22   C. 5   D. √29

20. Given the following front and top view of a solid object, the right side view is   20._____

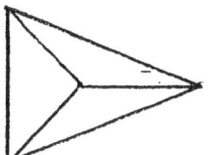
Top View

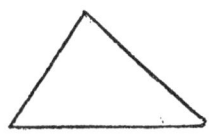
Front View   Right side View

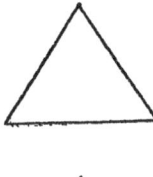   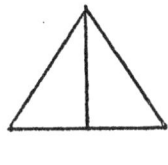   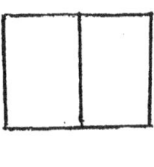   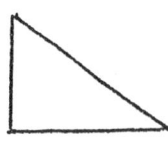

A   B   C   D

21. Given the following front and top view of a solid object, the right side view is   21._____

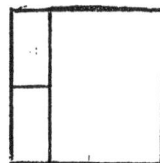
Top View

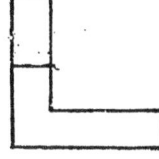      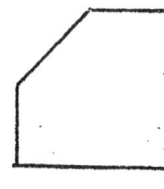   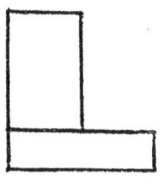   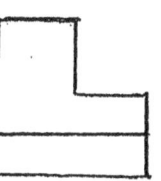

Front View   A   B   C   D

22. The bearing of line EF is S42°-18'-20"E, and the bearing of line FG is S11°-39'-10"E. Angle EFG is equal to
    A. 149°-10'-50"   B. 30°-39'-10"   C. 153°-57'-30"   D. 137°-41'-40"

23.

    Angle E is equal to
    A. 48°   B. 49°   C. 50°   D. 51°

24. A decimeter is one _____ of a meter.

    A. tenth
    B. hundredth
    C. thousandth
    D. ten-thousandth

25. One second expressed as a decimal of a degree is equal to
    A. .028   B. .0028   C. .00028   D. .000028

KEY (CORRECT ANSWERS)

1.	D	11.	D
2.	C	12.	A
3.	B	13.	A
4.	B	14.	A
5.	A	15.	B
6.	C	16.	D
7.	A	17.	B
8.	B	18.	A
9.	C	19.	B
10.	B	20.	B

21. B
22. A
23. D
24. A
25. C

EXAMINATION SECTION
TEST 1

DIRECTIONS: Each question or incomplete statement is followed by several suggested answers or completions. Select the one that BEST answers the question or completes the statement. *PRINT THE LETTER OF THE CORRECT ANSWER IN THE SPACE AT THE RIGHT.*

1. One radian is, in degrees, MOST NEARLY

    A. 57.0000   B. 57.1960   C. 57.2055   D. 57.2958

2. One minute of arc results in an offset in 100 feet of _____ feet.

    A. .01   B. .02   C. .03   D. .04

3. A distance is given as 501.05'. This distance is 501 feet and _____ inches.

    A. one-half   B. five-eighths
    C. three-quarters   D. seven-eighths

4. The number of square feet in a parcel of land is 41,625 square feet. The area of this parcel, in acres, is

    A. .936   B. .946   C. .956   D. .966

5. A measurement is made with an accuracy of (5 mm + 5 ppm). The accuracy of a 1000 meter measurement would be _____ mm.

    A. 10   B. 15   C. 20   D. 25

6. In the equation $\hat{\sigma}^2 = \frac{1}{n-1}\Sigma(x-\bar{x})^2$, $\hat{\sigma}^2$ is known as the

    A. sample variance   B. standard deviation
    C. sample mean   D. error of propagation

7. In aerial photogrammetry, the intervalometer

    A. sets the time between exposures
    B. controls the intensity of light received by the camera
    C. keeps the axis of the camera vertical
    D. controls the size of the photograph taken

8. In aerial photogrammetry, the v/H computer may be used to

    A. determine the optimal height for the photograph
    B. determine the optimal velocity for the photograph
    C. set the time interval between exposures
    D. locate ground reference points

9. The instantaneous field of view of the optics determines the area of the element on the ground that is imaged on a single detector. This is referred to as a

    A. push broom   B. raster
    C. pixel   D. strip

10. In vertical aerial photography with a square format, the size of the aerial photograph is usually

    A. 8" x 8" B. 9" x 9" C. 10" x 10" D. 11" x 11"

11. Overlap of aerial photographs is usually about

    A. 30% B. 4.0% C. 50% D. 60%

12. In Lambert conformal conic projection, the scale for parallels is exact for _____ parallel(s).

    A. one B. two C. four D. all

13. True North can be found astronomically with relative ease by sighting of the star

    A. deneb
    B. ursa minor
    C. polaris
    D. vega

14. Geoid is

    A. a hypothetical image of the surface of the earth where the section taken through the North-South axis is a circle
    B. the earth viewed as a hypothetical ellipsoid
    C. a hypothetical of the surface of the earth and each latitude is an ellipse
    D. where the latitudes and longitudes are elliptic curves

15. Longitudes are expressed either in degrees of arc or hours of time. One hour of time is equal to _____ degrees.

    A. 5 B. 10 C. 15 D. 20

16. On the celestial sphere, comparable to the parallels of latitude, are the parallels of

    A. right ascension
    B. nutation
    C. declination
    D. precession

17. In astronomical surveying, the complement of the altitude is the

    A. azimuth distance
    B. meridian distance
    C. celestial bearing
    D. zenith distance

18. EDM is used in measuring

    A. vertical angles
    B. horizontal angles
    C. distances
    D. positions of latitude and longitude

19. The Tellurometer sends signals by

    A. light pulses
    B. microwave
    C. laser
    D. infrared

20. Most electronic distance measuring instruments use

    A. infrared emission
    B. white light emission
    C. ultraviolet emission
    D. microwave

21. A millimicrosecond in scientific notation is 10 to the _____ power.   21____
    A. -7   B. -8   C. -9   D. -10

22. The Greek symbol for wavelength is   22____
    A. delta   B. kappa   C. lambda   D. rho

23. The frequency of the lightwave is measured in   23____
    A. cps   B. mps   C. nps   D. rps

24. The velocity of light in air V is equal to $V = V_O/n$, where V_O is the velocity of light in a vacuum and n is the   24____
    A. coefficient of resistance
    B. refractive index of light
    C. reflection number of air
    D. resistance number of air

25. The velocity of light in air varies with a change in atmospheric pressure   25____
    A. only
    B. and air temperature
    C. , air temperature, and humidity
    D. , air temperature, humidity, and turbidity

KEY (CORRECT ANSWERS)

1. D   11. D
2. C   12. B
3. B   13. C
4. C   14. B
5. A   15. C

6. A   16. C
7. A   17. D
8. C   18. C
9. C   19. B
10. B   20. A

21. C
22. C
23. A
24. B
25. C

TEST 2

DIRECTIONS: Each question or incomplete statement is followed by several suggested answers or completions. Select the one that BEST answers the question or completes the statement. *PRINT THE LETTER OF THE CORRECT ANSWER IN HE SPACE AT THE RIGHT.*

1. A millionth of a thousand meters is _____ millimeter(s).　　1____

   A. .01   B. .1   C. 1   D. 10

2. A 100 foot steel tape will expand with a 30 degree Fahrenheit change in temperature _____ foot.　　2____

   A. .01   B. .02   C. .03   D. .04

3. The length of a surveyor's (or Gunther's) chain is _____ feet.　　3____

   A. 60   B. 62   C. 64   D. 66

4. The effect of curvature and refraction is c & r = $0.57M^2$, where M is the distance in miles and C & F is in feet. Station E has an elevation of 95.16' and is 50 feet from the level. Station F is a half-mile from the level. If the backsight on Sta E is 5.67' and the foresight on Sta F is 7.21', the true elevation of Sta F is　　4____

   A. 93.76   B. 93.90   C. 94.04   D. 94.18

5. Pacing to determine the length of a line is MOST likely used　　5____

   A. to insure there are no obstacles in measuring the distance
   B. as a rough method to check for large errors in measuring distance
   C. to determine the length of your pace
   D. as a rough method to locate existing monuments

6. A plat is the same as a　　6____

   A. topographic map　　B. map of a traverse
   C. plot plan　　D. route map

7. Whenever the transit is being carried, the lower clamp screws should be clamped　　7____

   A. with moderate tightness
   B. very lightly
   C. tightly
   D. tightly or loosely, depending on the terrain

8. One hectare is equal to _____ square meters.　　8____

   A. 10   B. 100   C. 1,000   D. 10,000

9. In general, public lands have been divided into townships, bounded by meridianal and latitudinal lines. Each township is _____ square miles.　　9____

   A. 3   B. 4   C. 5   D. 6

10. The United States Army Corps of Engineers maps are a valuable source of information for

    A. United States pier and bulkhead line surveys and maps
    B. maps of streams
    C. maps of property owned by the United States government
    D. records of patents and early deeds

11. The Office of General Services Bureau of Surplus Real Property has information related not only to surplus property but also to

    A. property owned as state parks
    B. maps of land under water
    C. property owned as armories
    D. maps of easements

12. Municipal tax offices are a valuable source relating pririarily to

    A. owners' names
    B. liens
    C. property held in escrow
    D. municipal land

13. The State Department of Taxation and Finance, Mortgages, and Finance Bureau is a valuable source of

    A. maps showing turnpike locations
    B. patent maps
    C. maps showing canal locations
    D. unrecorded maps

14. Abstracts of title acquired for state acquisition purposes are made to cover a period of _____ years.

    A. 40   B. 50   C. 60   D. 70

15. It is customary with many surveyors to omit from the plan certain data such as angles or bearings yet still fulfill the purpose for which it was made. The reason for this is

    A. when the tract is resurveyed, it will act as a check on the original survey
    B. only salient information is needed for the survey
    C. when the tract is resurveyed, only the original surveyor will have the necessary data to do the job
    D. this information is usually optional

16. On a topographic map with contours, the natural feature that gives much information regarding the positioning of contours are

    A. valleys   B. hills   C. streams   D. sinkholes

17. On a topographic map showing the drainage area for a dam, the line enclosing the drainage area would be a

    A. contour of the maximum height in the drainage area
    B. line showing the maximum slope in the drainage area
    C. ridge line
    D. valley line

18. The contour crossing a street would appear as in

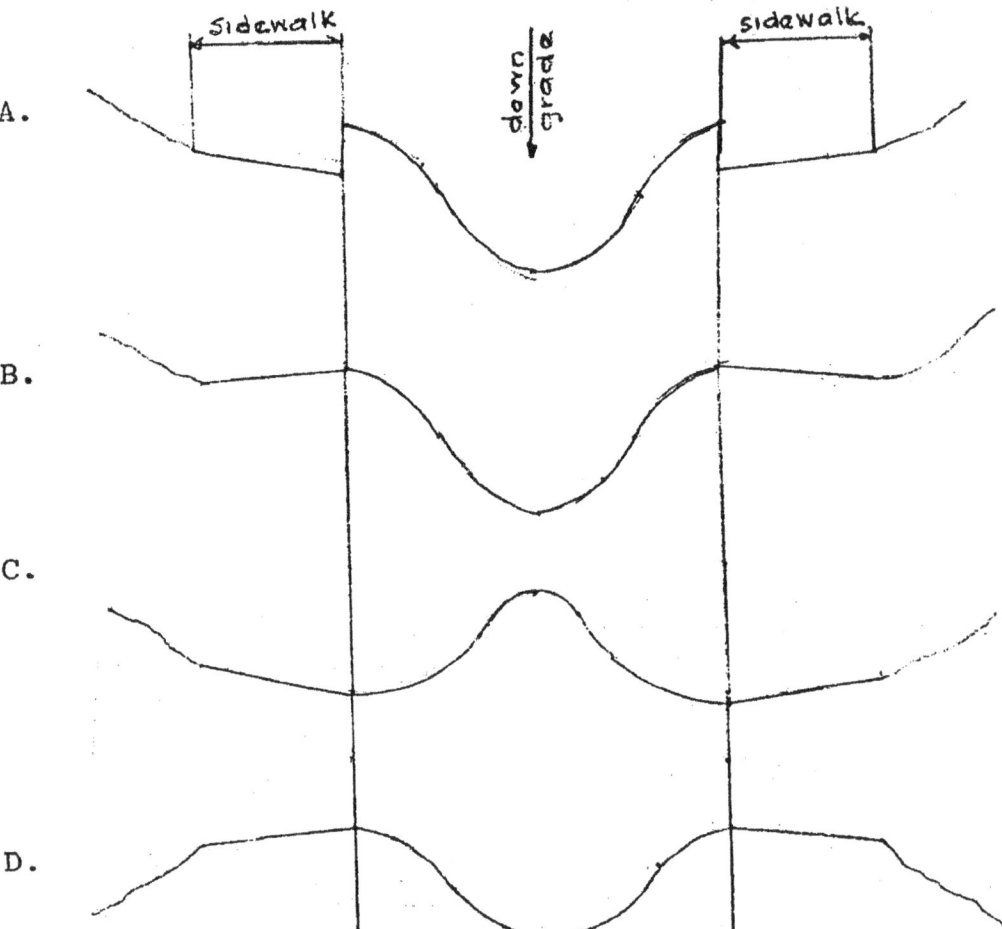

19.

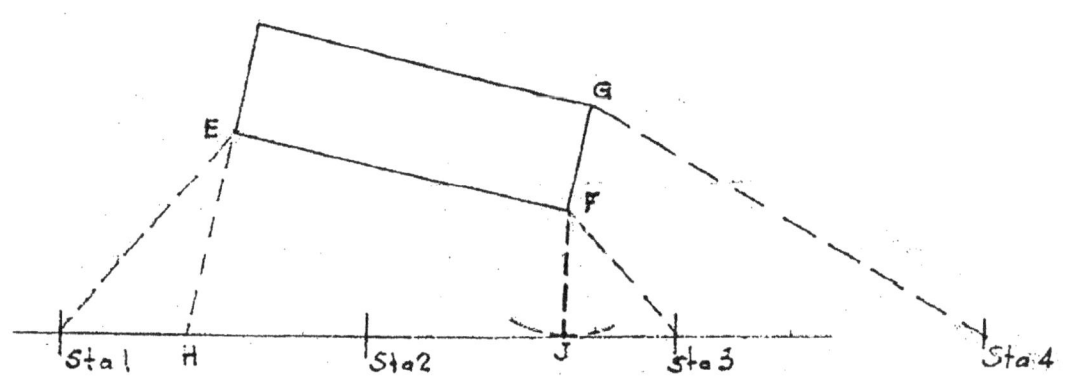

In locating a building in relation to a transit line, the line that is a range line is

A. EH
B. FJ
C. F - Sta 3
D. G - Sta 4

20. One hectare is equal to _____ acres.   20____

    A. 1.47 B. 2.47 C. 3.47 D. 4.47

21. An example of tacheometry is   21____

    A. traversing with transit
    B. stadia with transit
    C. reciprocal level with transit
    D. geodetic surveying with theodolite

22. The sura of the angles in a closed polygon is, in degrees, 180   22____

    A. n B. (n-1) C. (n-2) D. (n-3)

23. One meter equals _____ feet.   23____

    A. 3.28 B. 3.27 C. 3.26 D. 3.25

24. The trade name for the material composition of steel tapes used in high precision surveying is   24____

    A. invar B. covar C. novar D. unvar

25. A tribrach on a repeating theodolite consists of the   25____

    A. standard and the telescope
    B. alidade and the standard
    C. horizontal circle and the standard
    D. leveling head and baseplate

KEY (CORRECT ANSWERS)

1. C   11. B
2. B   12. A
3. D   13. B
4. A   14. A
5. B   15. C

6. C   16. C
7. B   17. C
8. D   18. A
9. D   19. A
10. A   20. B

21. B
22. C
23. A
24. A
25. D

EXAMINATION SECTION
TEST 1

DIRECTIONS: Each question or incomplete statement is followed by several suggested answers or completions. Select the one that BEST answers the question or completes the statement. *PRINT THE LETTER OF THE CORRECT ANSWER IN THE SPACE AT THE RIGHT.*

1. The basic quantum unit of a two-dimensional computer image is a

    A. bit   B. zel   C. bitmap   D. pixel

2. Noise reduction in a computer image can be accomplished to some degree by

    A. increasing the spatial resolution
    B. using a low-pass filter
    C. image averaging
    D. dissolving the image

3. The specialized memory used for storing bitmaps and displaying them on screen is called the

    A. display list memory   B. operand
    C. video card   D. buffer

4. In computer graphics, the popular *process* color model uses each of the following color channels EXCEPT

    A. black   B. red   C. cyan   D. magenta

5. Which of the following is a specialized computer language for two-dimensional page description?

    A. RenderMan   B. PostScript
    C. Phigs   D. Freehand

6. Which of the following peripheral devices is used as a zel scanning input device?

    A. Shaft encoder   B. NMR scanner
    C. Raster radar   D. CAT scan

7. The purpose of a zel is to

    A. convert an analog image to a digital computerized medium
    B. represent luminance at each point in an image
    C. sample a particular area of an analog image for later digital conversion
    D. store three-dimensional information in two-dimensional bitplanes

8. What is the term for the rotation of an image around its horizontal axis?

    A. Yaw   B. Roll   C. Pitch   D. Slope

9. The PRIMARY disadvantage associated with a *placed* destination document is that the

    A. component files are not actually copied to the destination document
    B. document must be updated if there are changes to any of its component pieces
    C. pointer copied along with component documents is often inaccurate
    D. destination document is not actually complete or integral

121

10. An inventory of a computer image, which presents the number of pixels at each intensity value in graphic form, is known as a(n)

    A. histogram
    B. frame buffer
    C. matte
    D. look-up table

11. A graphic preprocessor is an extension of the

    A. operand
    B. interpreter
    C. assembly language
    D. compiler

12. The purpose of *instancing* an image is to

    A. produce an analog sequence of animation
    B. displacing two axes of an image against a third axis
    C. repeat the occurrence of a visual object in many positions within an image
    D. represent a three-dimensional image on a monitor or sheet of paper

13. What is the term for the number of pixels used to represent an image from top to bottom and from right to left?

    A. Saturation
    B. Spatial resolution
    C. Intensity resolution
    D. Dynamic range

14. Each of the following is an input peripheral that could be used in 3D point imaging EXCEPT

    A. data glove
    B. sonar
    C. flying spot scanner
    D. laser measuring tool

15. In order to reduce the *jaggies* of a computer image, which of the following would be MOST effective?

    A. Decrease dynamic range
    B. Use a high-pass filter
    C. Adjust luminance
    D. Increase spatial resolution

16. The purpose of occultation in computer graphics is to

    A. determine the edges and surfaces of an image that would be visible from an observer's point of view
    B. provide a dynamic graphic feel that will simulate streak photography
    C. represent opaque surfaces with a range of dark to light values
    D. draws more distant lines with a dot pattern or a darker value

17. A four-dimensional representation of a three-dimensional object across time is known as

    A. planar manipulation
    B. space-time
    C. volumetric representation
    D. animation

18. Which of the following is a 2D pixel input peripheral?

    A. Laser drum scanner
    B. Light pen
    C. Touch screen
    D. Trackball

19. Which of the following is a specialized computer language for forming three-dimensional objects? 19.____

    A. RenderMan   B. PostScript
    C. Phigs   D. Logo

20. Which of the following is the PUREST method for color representation in a display or output? 20.____

    A. Composite color   B. Process color
    C. Component color   D. Multispectral imaging

21. The discrete quantum unit of a three-dimensional computer image is a 21.____

    A. voxel   B. normal   C. volume   D. zel

22. Which of the following techniques produces the visual image of contoured areas of color in what was originally a black-and-white image? 22.____

    A. Tint   B. Dithering
    C. Pseudocolor   D. Conversion

23. A common problem in converting analog images to digital representations is the loss of information resulting from insufficient or poorly integrated image samples. This is known as 23.____

    A. aliasing   B. blanking
    C. quantization   D. noise

24. What type of destination document stores only a pointer at the destination, and does not include the actual component files? 24.____

    A. Embedded   B. Linked
    C. Distributed   D. Placed

25. What is the term for the rotation of an image around its direction of travel through the visual field? 25.____

    A. Yaw   B. Roll   C. Pitch   D. Slope

KEY (CORRECT ANSWERS)

1. D
2. B
3. C
4. B
5. B

6. C
7. D
8. C
9. B
10. A

11. D
12. C
13. B
14. C
15. D

16. A
17. D
18. A
19. A
20. C

21. A
22. C
23. A
24. B
25. B

TEST 2

DIRECTIONS: Each question or incomplete statement is followed by several suggested answers or completions. Select the one that BEST answers the question or completes the statement. *PRINT THE LETTER OF THE CORRECT ANSWER IN THE SPACE AT THE RIGHT.*

1. Which type of specialized rendering of an object allows the observer to view an image "dead on"? _____ projection.

    A. orthogonal
    B. axonometric
    C. oblique
    D. perspective

2. Which of the following is a means for defining two-dimensional locations in terms of an angle and a radius?

    A. Orthogonal distances
    B. Polar coordinates
    C. Cartesian coordinates
    D. Altazimuthal coordinates

3. The output for voxel input devices would MOST likely take the form of

    A. stereo lithography
    B. a printer
    C. a vibrating display
    D. a video raster CRT

4. The orientation of a three-dimensional computer image's surface is described by the direction it is facing, or its

    A. vector
    B. pitch
    C. stellation
    D. normal

5. The HLS color model is useful in computer graphics because

    A. the gray level will automatically change in proportion to adjustments in saturation
    B. it allows transparent composite images to show through
    C. it permits luminance to be manipulated as a variable independent of hue and saturation
    D. it permits the application of multispectral imaging

6. The number of frames or points that can be displayed per second by a peripheral system is expressed in terms of

    A. luminance
    B. spatial resolution
    C. saturation
    D. temporal resolution

7. What is the term for a pixel array that is smaller than the total area of a picture, and which functions as a submodule?

    A. Cell
    B. Strobe
    C. Sprite
    D. Matte

8. A _____ is a pixel input peripheral that will record images as pixels directly onto a floppy disk.

    A. flat bed scanner
    B. video still camera
    C. photogram
    D. video scanner

1.____
2.____
3.____
4.____
5.____
6.____
7.____
8.____

9. The number of horizontal pixels in an image, divided by the number of vertical pixels, will produce the image's

   A. aspect ratio
   B. slope
   C. raster
   D. resolution

10. Which of the following techniques is used to maintain the total color information of an image while representing it with fewer colors?

    A. Tint
    B. Dithering
    C. Pseudocolor
    D. Conversion

11. The MOST common spatial-aliasing effect encountered in computer-generated images is

    A. noise
    B. blanking
    C. jaggies
    D. moire pattern

12. The number of dots in a computer image is expressed in terms of

    A. luminance
    B. spatial resolution
    C. saturation
    D. temporal resolution

13. The MAIN difference between drop shadows and extrusions is that

    A. extrusions extend into space and are three-dimensional
    B. drop shadows are concerned only with vertical axes
    C. extrusions are instanced to a greater extent
    D. drop shadows are used for 3D imaging only

14. The entire matrix of pixels in an image is known as the

    A. bitplane
    B. array
    C. bitmap
    D. tessellation

15. What is the term for a bitmap that records the transparency of an image at each pixel?

    A. Alpha channel
    B. Matte
    C. Operand
    D. Composite

16. Which of the following is a specialized computer program for manipulating two-dimensional images?

    A. Freehand
    B. QuickDraw
    C. Photoshop
    D. Phigs

17. Which of the following is NOT classified as a *subtractive* primary color?

    A. Yellow
    B. Orange
    C. Magenta
    D. Cyan

18. What type of destination document stores both the component files and a pointer to each of the source applications?

    A. Embedded
    B. Linked
    C. Distributed
    D. Placed

19. Which of the following techniques enlarges or reduces the number of pixels that define an image?

    A. Scan conversion
    B. Scaling
    C. Scrolling
    D. Spatial resolution

20. Which of the following is a means for defining three-dimensional locations in terms of two angles and one magnitude?

    A. Orthogonal distances
    B. Polar coordinates
    C. Cartesian coordinates
    D. Altazimuthal coordinates

21. Each of the following is an output peripheral that can be used in 2D pixel imaging EXCEPT a

    A. dot matrix printer
    B. multiplex hologram
    C. thermal wax plotter
    D. film recorder

22. Which of the following is a function of how many bits are stored in each pixel of an image?

    A. Spatial resolution
    B. Contrast
    C. Dynamic range
    D. Saturation

23. What is the term for the rotation of an image around its vertical axis?

    A. Yaw
    B. Roll
    C. Pitch
    D. Slope

24. A(n) _____ projection is a type of specialized rendering of an object which scales distances along three axes.

    A. orthogonal
    B. isometric
    C. oblique
    D. perspective

25. The number of gray levels or colors in an image is expressed in terms of

    A. luminance
    B. spatial resolution
    C. saturation
    D. temporal resolution

KEY (CORRECT ANSWERS)

1. A
2. B
3. A
4. D
5. C

6. D
7. C
8. B
9. A
10. B

11. C
12. B
13. A
14. C
15. B

16. C
17. B
18. A
19. B
20. B

21. B
22. C
23. A
24. B
25. A

EXAMINATION SECTION
TEST 1

DIRECTIONS: Each question or incomplete statement is followed by several suggested answers or completions. Select the one that BEST answers the question or completes the statement. *PRINT THE LETTER OF THE CORRECT ANSWER IN THE SPACE AT THE RIGHT.*

1. Computer graphic programming is concerned with　　　　　　　　　　　　　　　　1._____
   A. animation　　　　　　　　　　　　B. pixel addressing
   C. color representation　　　　　　　D. all of the above

2. DIB is an abbreviation for　　　　　　　　　　　　　　　　　　　　　　　　　　2._____
   A. data input button　　　　　　　　B. data dependent bitmap
   C. device independent bitmap　　　D. none of the above

3. Computer graphics can be categorized into　　　　　　　　　　　　　　　　　　3._____
   A. real time　　　　　　　　　　　　B. interactive
   C. photo-realistic　　　　　　　　　D. all of the above

4. DIB are used as native graphics for　　　　　　　　　　　　　　　　　　　　　4._____
   A. Windows Embedded CE　　　　　B. Directx
   C. both A and B　　　　　　　　　　D. none of the above

5. An image is _____ of pixel which varies in colors.　　　　　　　　　　　　　　　5._____
   A. triangle　　　　　　　　　　　　　B. rectangle
   C. circle　　　　　　　　　　　　　　D. all of the above

6. Graphic software deals with　　　　　　　　　　　　　　　　　　　　　　　　　6._____
   A. images　　　　　　　　　　　　　B. animations
   C. architecture　　　　　　　　　　　D. all of the above

7. Skencil is a program which is developed for　　　　　　　　　　　　　　　　　7._____
   A. Unix　　　　　　　　　　　　　　B. Linux
   C. none of the above　　　　　　　　D. both A and B

8. 3D Plus is suitable for _____ jobs.　　　　　　　　　　　　　　　　　　　　　8._____
   A. small　　　　　　　　　　　　　　B. quick
   C. long　　　　　　　　　　　　　　D. all of the above

9. An important characteristic of digital cameras is　　　　　　　　　　　　　　　9._____
   A. speed　　　　　　　　　　　　　　B. portability
   C. non-contact digitizing　　　　　　D. all of the above

10. Snap is a function of AutoCAD which is used to _____ fixed points.
    A. add
    B. delete
    C. maintain
    D. all of the above

11. Engineering drawings include
    A. isometric
    B. orthographic
    C. dimensioning
    D. all of the above

12. Drafting is another name of _____ drawing.
    A. technical
    B. engineering
    C. complex
    D. all of the above

13. Architectural models represent _____ design.
    A. technical
    B. engineering
    C. architectural
    D. none of the above

14. Base maps represent physical features like
    A. street grids
    B. river locations
    C. landscapes
    D. all of the above

15. Two major types of base maps are
    A. skeleton base maps
    B. country and township base maps
    C. interior maps
    D. A and B only

16. Abstraction is the most important phase in the _____ process.
    A. development
    B. design
    C. both A and B
    D. none of the above

17. In the design process, _____ helps in redesigning.
    A. abstraction
    B. models
    C. simulation
    D. all of the above

18. Prerequisites for logical design are
    A. business analysis
    B. technical requirements
    C. both A and B
    D. none of the above

19. A graphics technician maintains records in the form of
    A. print orders
    B. billing files
    C. maintenance agreements
    D. all of the above

20. Technical drawing requires intensive
    A. communication
    B. expertise
    C. both A and B
    D. none of the above

21. A computer graphic technician is responsible for
    A. concepts
    B. interpretation of design
    C. both A and B
    D. none of the above

22. A computer graphic technician deals with
    A. advertising
    B. marketing
    C. multimedia publishing
    D. all of the above

    22._____

23. A graphic technician should have communication with a
    A. graphic designer
    B. requirement engineer
    C. project manager
    D. all of the above

    23._____

24. Interdisciplinary environment is important for a
    A. graphic technician
    B. graphic designer
    C. none of the above
    D. both A and B

    24._____

25. A graphic technician must be
    A. a team player
    B. challenging
    C. innovative
    D. all of the above

    25._____

KEY (CORRECT ANSWERS)

1.	D		11.	D
2.	C		12.	A
3.	D		13.	C
4.	C		14.	D
5.	B		15.	D
6.	D		16.	B
7.	D		17.	C
8.	A		18.	C
9.	D		19.	D
10.	A		20.	A

21. C
22. D
23. D
24. A
25. D

TEST 2

DIRECTIONS: Each question or incomplete statement is followed by several suggested answers or completions. Select the one that BEST answers the question or completes the statement. *PRINT THE LETTER OF THE CORRECT ANSWER IN THE SPACE AT THE RIGHT.*

1. Visual unity is a basic goal for _____ design.   1.____
   A. graphic   B. web
   C. architecture   D. both A and B

2. _____ is an important element of good graphic design.   2.____
   A. color   B. hierarchy
   C. image   D. all of the above

3. Graphics designing is based on _____ of design.   3.____
   A. elements   B. principles
   C. none of the above   D. both A and B

4. Normally there are _____ elements of design.   4.____
   A. 5   B. 2
   C. 6   D. none of the above

5. Proximity is part of _____ of design.   5.____
   A. principles   B. elements
   C. none of the above   D. both A and B

6. Computer graphics can be divided into _____ groups.   6.____
   A. 2   B. 6   C. 5   D. 3

7. The basic shapes used in graphic design are   7.____
   A. circle   B. square
   C. triangle   D. all of the above

8. Positive and negative space must be considered in every   8.____
   A. concept   B. design
   C. element   D. none of the above

9. _____ is the critical aspect of graphic design.   9.____
   A. Size   B. Shape
   C. Color   D. None of the above

10. Graphical representations are _____ of textual content.   10.____
    A. images   B. illustrations
    C. both A and B   D. all of the above

132

11. An architectural model is a(n) _____ model.
    A. engineering
    B. complex
    C. scale
    D. all of the above

12. Presentation, fundraising, and obtaining permits can be shown by a(n) _____ model.
    A. software
    B. engineering
    C. architectural
    D. all of the above

13. Urban models are one of the _____ models.
    A. engineering
    B. scientific
    C. architectural
    D. none of the above

14. In industry and engineering, ideas are represented by
    A. design
    B. images
    C. technical drawings
    D. none of the above

15. Computer aided designs are of _____ types.
    A. five
    B. two
    C. three
    D. none of the above

16. _____ graphics are the easy way to present complex technical information.
    A. technical
    B. simple
    C. complex
    D. all of the above

17. _____ is an architecture design software.
    A. Photoshop
    B. Sketch Up
    C. None of the above
    D. Both A and B

18. Translating complex drawings into creative models is a(n) _____ task.
    A. challenging
    B. innovative
    C. important
    D. all of the above

19. Drawing tools assist in
    A. layout
    B. speed
    C. both A and B
    D. none of the above

20. Technical drawings can BEST be drawn by
    A. Autodesk
    B. Softimage
    C. both A and B
    D. none of the above

21. A graphic technician must have _____ skills.
    A. technical
    B. design
    C. both A and B
    D. none of the above

22. Information communication can help in resolving complex _____ issues.
    A. design
    B. technical
    C. architectural
    D. all of the above

23. A graphic technician collaborates with   23.____
    A. a team   B. stakeholders
    C. technical persons   D. all of the above

24. _____ are also prepared by a graphic technician.   24.____
    A. Presentations   B. Bitmap
    C. None of the above   D. Both A and B

25. A graphic technician works under the supervision of 25.____
    A. an engineer   B. architect
    C. graphic supervisor   D. all of the above

KEY (CORRECT ANSWERS)

1.	A	11.	C
2.	B	12.	C
3.	D	13.	C
4.	C	14.	C
5.	A	15.	B
6.	A	16.	B
7.	D	17.	B
8.	B	18.	D
9.	C	19.	C
10.	A	20.	A

21. C
22. D
23. D
24. A
25. C

TEST 3

DIRECTIONS: Each question or incomplete statement is followed by several suggested answers or completions. Select the one that BEST answers the question or completes the statement. *PRINT THE LETTER OF THE CORRECT ANSWER IN THE SPACE AT THE RIGHT.*

1. Graphic representations include
    A. concept maps
    B. comparison
    C. process
    D. all of the above

    1.____

2. Similarity is an important concern of design
    A. principle
    B. web designer
    C. computer graphic technician
    D. A and B only

    2.____

3. 3D computer graphics depend on _____ images.
    A. raster
    B. vector
    C. bitmap
    D. both A and B

    3.____

4. A three-dimensional object can be represented by a(n) _____ model.
    A. 3D
    B. technical
    C. engineering
    D. all of the above

    4.____

5. _____ is the best way to convert a model into an image.
    A. Drafting
    B. Rendering
    C. Drawing
    D. All of the above

    5.____

6. 3D modeling software includes
    A. Blender
    B. Art of Illusion
    C. Softimage
    D. all of the above

    6.____

7. AutoCAD is concerned with
    A. drafting
    B. developing
    C. customizing
    D. all of the above

    7.____

8. To open a 2D drawing in a 3D program, _____ file extension works well.
    A. DWG
    B. GIF
    C. PNG
    D. all of the above

    8.____

9. Paper design is replaced by
    A. AutoCAD
    B. Microstation
    C. none of the above
    D. both A and B

    9.____

10. _____ demonstrates 2D and 3D modeling.
    A. Drafting
    B. Designing
    C. None of the above
    D. All of the above

    10.____

11. Architects use architectural models because models provide
    A. quick understanding
    B. efficiency
    C. easy demonstration
    D. all of the above
    11.____

12. Which of the following types of model is normally used for landscape modeling?
    A. Interior model
    B. Exterior model
    C. Urban model
    D. All of the above
    12.____

13. Prototyping technologies are normally _____ based.
    A. modeling
    B. Photoshop
    C. CAD
    D. all of the above
    13.____

14. In an isometric model, object lines are always drawn
    A. vertically
    B. horizontally
    C. parallel
    D. all of the above
    14.____

15. Hidden components of a device are shown by _____ through technical drawing.
    A. AutoCAD
    B. Cross-sectional view
    C. Both A and B
    D. none of the above
    15.____

16. A technical drawing has _____ basic applications.
    A. two
    B. five
    C. three
    D. none of the above
    16.____

17. Full section view in architectural design is known as
    A. dimension
    B. plan
    C. axis
    D. all of the above
    17.____

18. Engineering drawings are concerned with
    A. layout
    B. interpretation
    C. appearance
    A. all of the above
    18.____

19. Two types of technical drawings which are based on graphic projection are
    A. two-dimensional representation
    B. three-dimensional representation
    C. both A and B
    D. none of the above
    19.____

20. Interior models are concerned with
    A. space planning
    B. furniture
    C. colors
    D. all of the above
    20.____

21. A graphic technician should be aware of
    A. principles
    B. processes
    C. equipment
    D. all of the above
    21.____

22. Interpersonal skills are important to learn for 22._____
    A. graphics technician   B. web designer
    C. project manager   D. all of the above

23. Record keeping techniques are defined by 23._____
    A. stakeholders   B. graphic designers
    C. graphic technicians   D. all of the above

24. Maintenance of equipment is important to keep 24._____
    A. data   B. records
    C. none of the above   D. both A and B

25. _____ communication is an important concern of the design phase. 25._____
    A. Oral   B. Written
    C. Both A and B   D. None of the above

KEY (CORRECT ANSWERS)

1.	D		11.	D
2.	A		12.	B
3.	D		13.	C
4.	A		14.	A
5.	B		15.	B
6.	D		16.	A
7.	D		17.	B
8.	A		18.	D
9.	D		19.	C
10.	A		20.	D

21. D
22. D
23. C
24. B
25. D

TEST 4

DIRECTIONS: Each question or incomplete statement is followed by several suggested answers or completions. Select the one that BEST answers the question or completes the statement. *PRINT THE LETTER OF THE CORRECT ANSWER IN THE SPACE AT THE RIGHT.*

1. Design elements include
   - A. attributes
   - B. shapes
   - C. architecture
   - D. all of the above

   1.____

2. Tactile texture provides _____ dimensional impression of the surface.
   - A. two
   - B. three
   - C. one
   - D. all of the above

   2.____

3. Space is an important concern of design which includes
   - A. overlap
   - B. shading
   - C. highlight
   - D. all of the above

   3.____

4. Repetition and continuation are methods of _____ design.
   - A. elements
   - B. both A and C
   - C. principles
   - D. all of the above

   4.____

5. Direction and texture are _____ of design.
   - A. elements
   - B. rules
   - C. both A and B
   - D. all of the above

   5.____

6. Architecture design is handled through
   - A. CAD
   - B. CAAD
   - C. AutoCAD
   - D. all of the above

   6.____

7. _____ is used for 3D architecture of homes.
   - A. Photoshop
   - B. Autodesk
   - C. Chief architect
   - D. All of the above

   7.____

8. Autodesk has the ability to provide
   - A. innovation
   - B. visualization
   - C. simulation
   - D. all of the above

   8.____

9. Building information modeling is the modern drift in
   - A. architecture
   - B. engineering
   - C. construction
   - D. all of the above

   9.____

10. _____ is a software tool for business information modeling.
    - A. Archicad
    - B. AutoCAD
    - C. Illustrator
    - D. All of the above

    10.____

11. Home, kitchen, baths, and interiors are BEST designed by
    A. home designer suit
    B. Archicad
    C. both A and B
    D. all of the above

11.____

12. When CAD is used for mechanical designs, _____ based graphics are preferred.
    A. raster
    B. vector
    C. both A and B
    D. all of the above

12.____

13. CAD is also used in industrial
    A. aerospace
    B. automotives
    C. shipbuilding
    D. all of the above

13.____

14. Animations can also be created by using
    A. Photoshop
    B. CAD
    C. Flash
    D. all of the above

14.____

15. Photo simulations are prepared by using
    A. Photoshop
    B. CAD
    C. CAAD
    D. both A and B

15.____

16. 3D wireframe is an extension of _____ drafting.
    A. 2D
    B. 3D
    C. linear
    D. all of the above

16.____

17. AutoCAD software for 2D drafting provides
    A. customization
    B. quick design
    C. precise templates
    D. all of the above

17.____

18. _____ is concerned with design blueprints.
    A. CAD pro technical drawing
    B. Softimage
    C. Edraw
    D. None of the above

18.____

19. Speed, efficiency, and portability are benefits of
    A. AutoCAD
    B. CAD pro technical drawing
    C. both A and B
    D. none of the above

19.____

20. Detailed technical drawings always save
    A. time
    B. cost
    C. both A and B
    D. none of the above

20.____

21. Engineers and designers mostly use _____ to create 3D models.
    A. Solid Edge 2D Drafting
    B. Blender
    C. BRL-CAD
    D. none of the above

21.____

22. The most famous 2D CAD software is
    A. FreeCAD
    B. Photoshop
    C. AutoCAD
    D. all of the above

23. K3DSurf is used to draw
    A. mathematic models
    B. engineering
    C. architectural
    D. all of the above

24. Graphic technician concerns _____ to prepare designs.
    A. graphic designer
    B. technical persons
    C. team leaders
    D. all of the above

25. Patent designs are BEST handled by
    A. AutoCAD
    B. CAD Pro
    C. Blender
    D. all of the above

KEY (CORRECT ANSWERS)

1.	D		11.	A
2.	B		12.	B
3.	D		13.	D
4.	C		14.	D
5.	A		15.	B
6.	B		16.	A
7.	C		17.	D
8.	D		18.	A
9.	D		19.	B
10.	A		20.	C

21.	A
22.	C
23.	A
24.	D
25.	B

EXAMINATION SECTION

TEST 1

DIRECTIONS: Each question or incomplete statement is followed by several suggested answers or completions. Select the one that BEST answers the question or completes the statement. *PRINT THE LETTER OF THE CORRECT ANSWER IN THE SPACE AT THE RIGHT.*

1. Computer graphic programming is concerned with 1.____
   - A. animation
   - B. pixel addressing
   - C. color representation
   - D. all of the above

2. DIB is an abbreviation for 2.____
   - A. data input button
   - B. data dependent bitmap
   - C. device independent bitmap
   - D. none of the above

3. Computer graphics can be categorized into 3.____
   - A. real time
   - B. interactive
   - C. photo-realistic
   - D. all of the above

4. DIB are used as native graphics for 4.____
   - A. Windows Embedded CE
   - B. Directx
   - C. both A and B
   - D. none of the above

5. An image is _____ of pixel which varies in colors. 5.____
   - A. triangle
   - B. rectangle
   - C. circle
   - D. all of the above

6. Graphic software deals with 6.____
   - A. images
   - B. animations
   - C. architecture
   - D. all of the above

7. Skencil is a program which is developed for 7.____
   - A. Unix
   - B. Linux
   - C. none of the above
   - D. both A and B

8. 3D Plus is suitable for _____ jobs. 8.____
   - A. small
   - B. quick
   - C. long
   - D. all of the above

9. An important characteristic of digital cameras is 9.____
   - A. speed
   - B. portability
   - C. non-contact digitizing
   - D. all of the above

10. Snap is a function of AutoCAD which is used to _____ fixed points.
    A. add
    B. delete
    C. maintain
    D. all of the above

11. Engineering drawings include
    A. isometric
    B. orthographic
    C. dimensioning
    D. all of the above

12. Drafting is another name of _____ drawing.
    A. technical
    B. engineering
    C. complex
    D. all of the above

13. Architectural models represent _____ design.
    A. technical
    B. engineering
    C. architectural
    D. none of the above

14. Base maps represent physical features like
    A. street grids
    B. river locations
    C. landscapes
    D. all of the above

15. Two major types of base maps are
    A. skeleton base maps
    B. country and township base maps
    C. interior maps
    D. A and B only

16. Abstraction is the most important phase in the _____ process.
    A. development
    B. design
    C. both A and B
    D. none of the above

17. In the design process, _____ helps in redesigning.
    A. abstraction
    B. models
    C. simulation
    D. all of the above

18. Prerequisites for logical design are
    A. business analysis
    B. technical requirements
    C. both A and B
    D. none of the above

19. A graphics technician maintains records in the form of
    A. print orders
    B. billing files
    C. maintenance agreements
    D. all of the above

20. Technical drawing requires intensive
    A. communication
    B. expertise
    C. both A and B
    D. none of the above

21. A computer graphic technician is responsible for
    A. concepts
    B. interpretation of design
    C. both A and B
    D. none of the above

22. A computer graphic technician deals with
    A. advertising
    B. marketing
    C. multimedia publishing
    D. all of the above

    22.____

23. A graphic technician should have communication with a
    A. graphic designer
    B. requirement engineer
    C. project manager
    D. all of the above

    23.____

24. Interdisciplinary environment is important for a
    A. graphic technician
    B. graphic designer
    C. none of the above
    D. both A and B

    24.____

25. A graphic technician must be
    A. a team player
    B. challenging
    C. innovative
    D. all of the above

    25.____

KEY (CORRECT ANSWERS)

1.	D	11.	D
2.	C	12.	A
3.	D	13.	C
4.	C	14.	D
5.	B	15.	D
6.	D	16.	B
7.	D	17.	C
8.	A	18.	C
9.	D	19.	D
10.	A	20.	A

21. C
22. D
23. D
24. A
25. D

TEST 2

DIRECTIONS: Each question or incomplete statement is followed by several suggested answers or completions. Select the one that BEST answers the question or completes the statement. *PRINT THE LETTER OF THE CORRECT ANSWER IN THE SPACE AT THE RIGHT.*

1. Visual unity is a basic goal for _____ design. 1._____
   A. graphic
   B. web
   C. architecture
   D. both A and B

2. _____ is an important element of good graphic design. 2._____
   A. color
   B. hierarchy
   C. image
   D. all of the above

3. Graphics designing is based on _____ of design. 3._____
   A. elements
   B. principles
   C. none of the above
   D. both A and B

4. Normally there are _____ elements of design. 4._____
   A. 5
   B. 2
   C. 6
   D. none of the above

5. Proximity is part of _____ of design. 5._____
   A. principles
   B. elements
   C. none of the above
   D. both A and B

6. Computer graphics can be divided into _____ groups. 6._____
   A. 2   B. 6   C. 5   D. 3

7. The basic shapes used in graphic design are 7._____
   A. circle
   B. square
   C. triangle
   D. all of the above

8. Positive and negative space must be considered in every 8._____
   A. concept
   B. design
   C. element
   D. none of the above

9. _____ is the critical aspect of graphic design. 9._____
   A. Size
   B. Shape
   C. Color
   D. None of the above

10. Graphical representations are _____ of textual content. 10._____
    A. images
    B. illustrations
    C. both A and B
    D. all of the above

11. An architectural model is a(n) _____ model. 11._____
    A. engineering B. complex
    C. scale D. all of the above

12. Presentation, fundraising, and obtaining permits can be shown by a(n) _____ model. 12._____
    A. software B. engineering
    C. architectural D. all of the above

13. Urban models are one of the _____ models. 13._____
    A. engineering B. scientific
    C. architectural D. none of the above

14. In industry and engineering, ideas are represented by 14._____
    A. design B. images
    C. technical drawings D. none of the above

15. Computer aided designs are of _____ types. 15._____
    A. five B. two
    C. three D. none of the above

16. _____ graphics are the easy way to present complex technical information. 16._____
    A. technical B. simple
    C. complex D. all of the above

17. _____ is an architecture design software. 17._____
    A. Photoshop B. Sketch Up
    C. None of the above D. Both A and B

18. Translating complex drawings into creative models is a(n) _____ task. 18._____
    A. challenging B. innovative
    C. important D. all of the above

19. Drawing tools assist in 19._____
    A. layout B. speed
    C. both A and B D. none of the above

20. Technical drawings can BEST be drawn by 20._____
    A. Autodesk B. Softimage
    C. both A and B D. none of the above

21. A graphic technician must have _____ skills. 21._____
    A. technical B. design
    C. both A and B D. none of the above

22. Information communication can help in resolving complex _____ issues. 22._____
    A. design B. technical
    C. architectural D. all of the above

23. A graphic technician collaborates with 23.____
    A. a team B. stakeholders
    C. technical persons D. all of the above

24. _____ are also prepared by a graphic technician. 24.____
    A. Presentations B. Bitmap
    C. None of the above D. Both A and B

25. A graphic technician works under the supervision of 25.____
    A. an engineer B. architect
    C. graphic supervisor D. all of the above

KEY (CORRECT ANSWERS)

1.	A	11.	C
2.	B	12.	C
3.	D	13.	C
4.	C	14.	C
5.	A	15.	B
6.	A	16.	B
7.	D	17.	B
8.	B	18.	D
9.	C	19.	C
10.	A	20.	A

21.	C
22.	D
23.	D
24.	A
25.	C

TEST 3

DIRECTIONS: Each question or incomplete statement is followed by several suggested answers or completions. Select the one that BEST answers the question or completes the statement. *PRINT THE LETTER OF THE CORRECT ANSWER IN THE SPACE AT THE RIGHT.*

1. Graphic representations include
   A. concept maps
   B. comparison
   C. process
   D. all of the above

   1.____

2. Similarity is an important concern of design
   A. principle
   B. web designer
   C. computer graphic technician
   D. A and B only

   2.____

3. 3D computer graphics depend on _____ images.
   A. raster
   B. vector
   C. bitmap
   D. both A and B

   3.____

4. A three-dimensional object can be represented by a(n) _____ model.
   A. 3D
   B. technical
   C. engineering
   D. all of the above

   4.____

5. _____ is the best way to convert a model into an image.
   A. Drafting
   B. Rendering
   C. Drawing
   D. All of the above

   5.____

6. 3D modeling software includes
   A. Blender
   B. Art of Illusion
   C. Softimage
   D. all of the above

   6.____

7. AutoCAD is concerned with
   A. drafting
   B. developing
   C. customizing
   D. all of the above

   7.____

8. To open a 2D drawing in a 3D program, _____ file extension works well.
   A. DWG
   B. GIF
   C. PNG
   D. all of the above

   8.____

9. Paper design is replaced by
   A. AutoCAD
   B. Microstation
   C. none of the above
   D. both A and B

   9.____

10. _____ demonstrates 2D and 3D modeling.
    A. Drafting
    B. Designing
    C. None of the above
    D. All of the above

    10.____

147

11. Architects use architectural models because models provide
    A. quick understanding B. efficiency
    C. easy demonstration D. all of the above

    11._____

12. Which of the following types of model is normally used for landscape modeling?
    A. Interior model B. Exterior model
    C. Urban model D. All of the above

    12._____

13. Prototyping technologies are normally _____ based.
    A. modeling B. Photoshop
    C. CAD D. all of the above

    13._____

14. In an isometric model, object lines are always drawn
    A. vertically B. horizontally
    C. parallel D. all of the above

    14._____

15. Hidden components of a device are shown by _____ through technical drawing.
    A. AutoCAD B. Cross-sectional view
    C. Both A and B D. none of the above

    15._____

16. A technical drawing has _____ basic applications.
    A. two B. five
    C. three D. none of the above

    16._____

17. Full section view in architectural design is known as
    A. dimension B. plan
    C. axis D. all of the above

    17._____

18. Engineering drawings are concerned with
    A. layout B. interpretation
    C. appearance A. all of the above

    18._____

19. Two types of technical drawings which are based on graphic projection are
    A. two-dimensional representation B. three-dimensional representation
    C. both A and B D. none of the above

    19._____

20. Interior models are concerned with
    A. space planning B. furniture
    C. colors D. all of the above

    20._____

21. A graphic technician should be aware of
    A. principles B. processes
    C. equipment D. all of the above

    21._____

22. Interpersonal skills are important to learn for 22.____
    A. graphics technician B. web designer
    C. project manager D. all of the above

23. Record keeping techniques are defined by 23.____
    A. stakeholders B. graphic designers
    C. graphic technicians D. all of the above

24. Maintenance of equipment is important to keep 24.____
    A. data B. records
    C. none of the above D. both A and B

25. _____ communication is an important concern of the design phase. 25.____
    A. Oral B. Written
    C. Both A and B D. None of the above

KEY (CORRECT ANSWERS)

1.	D		11.	D
2.	A		12.	B
3.	D		13.	C
4.	A		14.	A
5.	B		15.	B
6.	D		16.	A
7.	D		17.	B
8.	A		18.	D
9.	D		19.	C
10.	A		20.	D

21. D
22. D
23. C
24. B
25. D

TEST 4

DIRECTIONS: Each question or incomplete statement is followed by several suggested answers or completions. Select the one that BEST answers the question or completes the statement. *PRINT THE LETTER OF THE CORRECT ANSWER IN THE SPACE AT THE RIGHT.*

1. Design elements include
   A. attributes
   B. shapes
   C. architecture
   D. all of the above

    1.____

2. Tactile texture provides _____ dimensional impression of the surface.
   A. two
   B. three
   C. one
   D. all of the above

    2.____

3. Space is an important concern of design which includes
   A. overlap
   B. shading
   C. highlight
   D. all of the above

    3.____

4. Repetition and continuation are methods of _____ design.
   A. elements
   B. both A and C
   C. principles
   D. all of the above

    4.____

5. Direction and texture are _____ of design.
   A. elements
   B. rules
   C. both A and B
   D. all of the above

    5.____

6. Architecture design is handled through
   A. CAD
   B. CAAD
   C. AutoCAD
   D. all of the above

    6.____

7. _____ is used for 3D architecture of homes.
   A. Photoshop
   B. Autodesk
   C. Chief architect
   D. All of the above

    7.____

8. Autodesk has the ability to provide
   A. innovation
   B. visualization
   C. simulation
   D. all of the above

    8.____

9. Building information modeling is the modern drift in
   A. architecture
   B. engineering
   C. construction
   D. all of the above

    9.____

10. _____ is a software tool for business information modeling.
    A. Archicad
    B. AutoCAD
    C. Illustrator
    D. All of the above

    10.____

11. Home, kitchen, baths, and interiors are BEST designed by   11.____
    A. home designer suit   B. Archicad
    C. both A and B   D. all of the above

12. When CAD is used for mechanical designs, _____ based graphics are   12.____
    preferred.
    A. raster   B. vector
    C. both A and B   D. all of the above

13. CAD is also used in industrial   13.____
    A. aerospace   B. automotives
    C. shipbuilding   D. all of the above

14. Animations can also be created by using   14.____
    A. Photoshop   B. CAD
    C. Flash   D. all of the above

15. Photo simulations are prepared by using   15.____
    A. Photoshop   B. CAD
    C. CAAD   D. both A and B

16. 3D wireframe is an extension of _____ drafting.   16.____
    A. 2D   B. 3D
    C. linear   D. all of the above

17. AutoCAD software for 2D drafting provides   17.____
    A. customization   B. quick design
    C. precise templates   D. all of the above

18. _____ is concerned with design blueprints.   18.____
    A. CAD pro technical drawing   B. Softimage
    C. Edraw   D. None of the above

19. Speed, efficiency, and portability are benefits of   19.____
    A. AutoCAD   B. CAD pro technical drawing
    C. both A and B   D. none of the above

20. Detailed technical drawings always save   20.____
    A. time   B. cost
    C. both A and B   D. none of the above

21. Engineers and designers mostly use _____ to create 3D models.   21.____
    A. Solid Edge 2D Drafting   B. Blender
    C. BRL-CAD   D. none of the above

22. The most famous 2D CAD software is
    A. FreeCAD
    B. Photoshop
    C. AutoCAD
    D. all of the above

23. K3DSurf is used to draw
    A. mathematic models
    B. engineering
    C. architectural
    D. all of the above

24. Graphic technician concerns _____ to prepare designs.
    A. graphic designer
    B. technical persons
    C. team leaders
    D. all of the above

25. Patent designs are BEST handled by
    A. AutoCAD
    B. CAD Pro
    C. Blender
    D. all of the above

KEY (CORRECT ANSWERS)

1.	D		11.	A
2.	B		12.	B
3.	D		13.	D
4.	C		14.	D
5.	A		15.	B
6.	B		16.	A
7.	C		17.	D
8.	D		18.	A
9.	D		19.	B
10.	A		20.	C

21.	A
22.	C
23.	A
24.	D
25.	B

GLOSSARY OF CAD/DRAFTING TERMS

2D plane: A flat, infinite 2D surface.

A

active standard: The standard that is currently in use in a model or drawing file.

aligned dimension: A dimension used to define an object or feature that is not vertical or horizontal.

alt-drag: Establishing assembly constraints, including mate, flush, tangent, and insert constraints, by dragging one component to another component; also called *drag-mate*.

angular dimension: A dimension used to define the angle between two lines.

arc: A circular curve in which all of the points are an equal distance from the center point.

arrowless dimensioning: A dimensioning method that provides coordinates from established datum's those are usually located at the corner of the part or the axis of a feature. Also called *rectangular coordinate dimensioning without dimension lines* or ordinate dimensioning.

assembly: A grouping of one or more design components.

assembly drawing: A 2D representation of an assembly.

assembly constraints: Constraints that establish geometric relationships and positions between one component face, edge, or axis and another component face, edge, or axis.

auxiliary view: A view used to show the true size and shape of an inclined surface that is not parallel to any of the projected views, including the front, top, bottom, left-side, right-side, and back views.

axis of rotation: The pivot point around which the selected geometry is copied.

B

balloon: A shape, usually circular, that is connected to an assembly component by a leader. It contains an identification number or letter that refers to an item in the parts list.

base environment: The overall working environment, within which secondary environments exist.

base feature: The initial model feature, on which all others are based.

baseline dimensioning: A dimensioning method in which the size and location of features are given in reference to a datum. Also referred to as *datum dimensioning*.

base view: The first view placed in a drawing, to which all other views are added.

bend radius: The inside radius of a formed feature.

bend relief: Relief typically added to a sheet metal part to relieve stress, or the tear, that occurs when a portion of a piece of material is bent.

bent: Formed using a brake, die, mandrel, roller, or similar tools.

border: A rectangle or polygon near the edge of the drawing sheet that defines the usable drawing area of the drawing sheet. Borders may also include zone numbers and center marks.

boundary patch: A surface formed by patching the space within a selected closed region.

bowtie grips: Handlebar endpoints used to adjust the shape of a spline.

browser bar (browser): A panel that displays all the items in the current model or drawing.

C

cascading menu: A secondary menu that contains options related to the chosen menu item.

catalog feature: A feature, part, or assembly stored in a catalog that can be inserted into a part model as a feature.

centerline: A line that defines an axis of symmetry or the center of a circular feature.

center of gravity: The center of model mass, where balance occurs.

center point: The intersection point of the X, Y, and Z axes in 3D space, or 0,0,0.

chamfers: Angled planar faces added to lines or curves. Angled planar faces placed on a feature edge.

child node: Subordinate nodes that create, are associated with, or are consumed by the parent node item.

circular feature pattern: Occurrences of features copied and positioned a specified distance apart around an axis.

circular pattern: An arrangement of copies of a feature around an imaginary circle, a designated number of times, and at a specified distance apart.

circumscribed: Describes a polygon in which the flats are tangent to an imaginary circle; circumscribed polygons are measured across the polygon flats.

closed loop: A sketch that is fully closed and does not contain any gaps or openings.

coil: A spiral, or helix, feature used primarily to create springs, detailed threads, and similar items.

coincident constraint: A constraint that forces two points to share the same location.

combs: Lines added to the spline to help illustrate and analyze the spline curvature.

components: The individual parts and subassemblies used to create an assembly.

composite iMates: Two or more iMates linked together and added to a single component; used for the same assembly operation.

constant fillets and rounds: Fillets and rounds that have a curve radius that does not change.

constraints: Parameters that control the size, location, and position of model elements, including sketches and features. Restrictions applied to sketches to define sketch geometry in reference to other sketch geometry. Also called *geometric constraints*.

construction geometry: Geometry used for construction purposes only. Inventor cannot use construction geometry to build sketched features.

consumed: Used up in the creation of a model or feature.

context-sensitive shortcut menu: Menu in which only items associated with the current work environment and application are available.

control keys: Shortcut key combinations that include the [Ctrl] key and a character key.

coordinate system: The system of XYZ coordinate values that defines the location of points in 3D space.

corner chamfers: Angled faces that replace square corners on sheet metal features.

corner relief: Relief typically added to a sheet metal part to relieve stress at a bend corner at the intersection of two or three faces.

corner rip: A feature that opens closed, usually square, corners.

corner round: A curve placed at an inside or outside sheet metal corner.

corner seams: Features that add or remove material to form a gap at sheet metal part corners. Corner seams create an appropriate corner transition for folding and to allow for unfolding.

counter bored hole: A drilled hole that has a larger-diameter cylindrical opening at the top; typically used when a flush surface is necessary, such as to hide a binding screw head.

countersunk hole: Similar to a counter bored hole, but the recess is tapered, resulting in a conical shape that is often used to hide a screw head.

curve: A straight or bent continuous object, such as a line, arc, spline, or circle.

cut: Remove volume from an existing extrusion by subtracting a new extrusion from it. Any process, such as shearing, punching, or laser, water jet, or similar process, used to remove material.

cutting-plane line: A line that represents the cutting plane of the section, which is the location where the view is sliced to show interior features.

cutting tool: A surface, quilt, 2D sketch curve, work plane or existing feature face intersecting the surface to trim that provides an edge to which the item is trimmed.

D

dangling geometry: A condition that results when additional positioning information is required in order for iFeature insertion to occur; primarily due to issues with the initial iFeature sketch and existing feature geometry.

database: A system that stores every model characteristic, including calculations, sketches, features, dimensions, geometric constraints, when each piece of the model was created, and all other model parameters and properties.

datum: A theoretically exact point, axis, or plane from which the location or geometric characteristics of features originate.

datum dimensioning: A dimensioning method in which the size and location of features are given in reference to a datum. Also referred to as *baseline dimensioning*.

decals: Images applied to a part or assembly to display information or decoratea product.

demote: Group more than one part in an assembly to create a subassembly.

dependents: Assembly component files referenced by the assembly.

dependent views: Views projected from and linked to another view, such as a base view.

derived components: Features that can contain a complete model consisting of several features, or even multiple parts; often used as a base feature. A saved part or assembly that can be inserted in a part as a feature.

design session: Time spent working on a project, including analyzing design parameters and using Inventor.

detail view: A view that shows a small, complex part feature at a larger scale.

dialog box: A window-like part of the user interface that contains various kinds of information and settings.

diameter: The distance across a circle from one side to the other through the center.

diameter dimension: A dimension used to define the diameter of a circle or circular object.

dimension: A measurement that numerically defines the size and location of sketch geometry, such as the length of a line, diameter of a circle, or radius of an arc. Specifications of the size and shape of object features so that parts can be manufactured; along with notes and other text, also specify the location and characteristics of geometry and surface texture.

docked: Describes interface items that are locked into position on an edge of the Inventor window (top, bottom, left, or right).

document units: The units used to define the linear, angular, time, and mass measurements and precision in models and drawings.

double bend: A bend between two parallel faces that are not coplanar.
drag-mate: Establishing assembly constraints, including mate, flush, tangent, and insert constraints, by dragging one component to another component; also called *alt-drag*.

drawing annotation tools: Tools that allow you to create annotations such as dimensions, notes, and other text on drawings.

drawing dimensions: Dimensions added to the drawing using Inventor's drawing annotation tools.

drawing sheet: A representation of the physical limits of the paper size on which the drawing will be printed.

drawings: 2D representations of models containing views, dimensions, and annotations.

drilled hole: The most basic hole type, with no counterbore, spotface, or countersink where the hole begins.

driven: Manipulated to see the amount of movement between components, pause movement, see adaptivity, and detect collisions between components.

driven dimension: A dimension used for reference purposes only. Reference dimensions are enclosed in parentheses to show that they are driven.

E

ellipse: An oval-like shape that contains both a major axis and a minor axis.

embossing: The process of raising shapes or text off the surface of an object that has volume, such as a block; the opposite of engraving.

engraving: The process of cutting into, or impressing, shapes or text into the surface of an object that has volume; the opposite of embossing.

external threads: Thread forms on an external feature such as a pin, shaft, bolt, or screw.

extrusion: A surface or solid that has a fixed cross-sectional profile determined by a sketch profile. The sketch profile is extended (extruded) along a linear path to create the 3D feature or part.

F

face draft: A taper placed on a part surface.

feature pattern: An arrangement of copied existing features, generating occurrences of the features. An arrangement of features in a specific pattern, or configuration; created using feature pattern tools.

fillets: Rounded interior corners; fillets add material to corners. A curve placed at the inside intersection of two or more faces, adding material to a feature.

flat angle: The number of degrees a coil end travels without pitch.

flat end: A type of coil end in which the first or last coil is adjusted to create a flat start or finish for the spring.)

flat pattern: A 2D drawing representing the final, unfolded part.

floating: Describes interface items, displayed within a border, that can be freely resized or moved.

flush solution: A constraint that positions two faces along the same plane, facing the same direction.

flyout: A button that presents additional, related tool buttons, much like a cascading menu.

fly-through: A viewing process that shows how it would look if you could fly in and around the actual product you are modeling.

frequently used subfolder: A virtual folder within a project that stores the paths to folders and files you use frequently.

fully constrained model: A model that has no freedom of movement.

full radius fillets and rounds: Fillets and rounds controlled by the linear dimension of a feature, such as the thickness of a part or width of a slot, producing half of a circle or cylinder; most often associated with a round.

G

general notes: Notes that apply to the entire drawing. General notes are usually placed together in the lower-left or upper-right corner of the drawing or in the title block.

geometric constraints: Restrictions applied to sketches to define sketch geometry in reference to other sketch geometry. Also called *constraints*.

geometric dimensioning and tolerancing (GD&T): The dimensioning and tolerancing of individual features of a part where the permissible variations relate to characteristics of form, profile, orientation, runout, or the location of features.

grab bars: Two thin bars at the top or left edge of a docked or floating item; used to move the item.

graphical user interface (GUI): On-screen interface items.

grounded component: An assembly component that is fixed in position, has no freedom of movement, and cannot be driven.

grounded work point: A work point completely fixed to an X, Y, Z coordinate at which it is placed.

guide rail: A 2D or 3D sketched curve that is used with the sweep path to manipulate and further control the shape of a sweep.

guide surface: A surface that helps control

the shape of a sweep along a complex path.

H

height: In a coil, the total depth of the coil from the center of the starting profile to the center of the ending profile.

help string: A short description of what happens if you select a tool or option over which the cursor is hovering, or if a tool is selected, a prompt indicating the appropriate action is shown.

hem: Flanges used to add strength to or relieve the sharpness of exposed edges, or to connect separate edges or parts together.

hot keys: Single character keys on the keyboard that allow you to access certain predefined tools.

I

icon: A small graphic representing an application, file, or tool.

i-drop: The process of dragging and dropping shared content into component files, or the tool used for this process.

iFeature: An existing feature or set of features you create and then save and store in a catalog to be used in other models. A stored feature that can be inserted in a part as a feature.

iMates: Constraints placed on an individual component that are later used for assembly.

included angle: The angle between two selected edges, curves, axes, faces, planes, or a combination of objects, such as an edge and a face.

included file: A separate project file linked to the current project.

increment: A set amount by which values increase in equal steps. For example, with an increment of 2, a size would increase to 4, 6, 8, 10, and so on.

inferred: Automatically detected using logic.

inscribed: Describes a polygon in which the corners touch an imaginary circle; inscribed polygons are measured from the corners.

interface: The tools and techniques used to provide information to and receive information from a computer application. Also called a *user interface*.

internal threads: Thread forms on an internal hole feature.

iProperties: Inventor file properties used to define a variety of file and design characteristics.

isometric view: A 3D view in which all three axes are shown at equal angles (120°) with the plane of projection.

J

join: Combine two or more existing features to create a single feature.

K

k-factor: A multiple, typically between .25 and .5, that locates the neutral axis.

L

leader: A line that connects the beginning or end of a note to the feature it describes. Leaders usually have a horizontal shoulder on the end nearest the text. The other end has an arrow pointing to the feature.

left-hand threads: Threads that move a left-hand threaded bolt forward in a counterclockwise direction.

library: A folder that contains files used in a project or several different projects.

library search paths: The locations in which Inventor looks for library files on the computer's hard drive or on the network.

linear dimension: A type of dimension used to define the vertical and horizontal size and location of object features.

local notes: Notes that apply to a specific feature or features on the drawing. Also called *specific notes*.

loft: A feature that references and blends two or more sections located on different planes.

loft centerline: A rail that acts as a path for blending sections along and symmetrically around the centerline sketch.

lump: Any set of external feature or surface faces created when you develop a solid model.

M

mate solution: A constraint that places two faces along the same plane facing in opposite directions, two axes collinear to each other, two edges collinear to each other, or two points matched together.

mirrored feature: mirrored features: A mirror image of an existing feature created symmetrically over a specified plane.

mirror plane: A plane of symmetry about which features are mirrored.

miter gap: Space between faces created during a corner seam or miter operation.

model dimensions: Dimensions that were used to create and constrain the model from which drawing content has been extracted.

modeling failure: The result of conflicting constraints that are impossible to apply to the model.

model parameters: Parameters that relate to the model. Model parameters are added when you insert a model view or add model information, such as dimensions.

model space: A space, or environment, in which the model defines the display orientation, regardless of the position of the model in the graphics window; the center is associated with the model pivot point.

monodetail drawing: A drawing of a single part on one sheet.

motion constraints: Assembly constraints that identify how movable components should move in reference to other movable components, using a specified ratio and direction.

multidetail drawing: A drawing of several parts on one sheet.

multiple document interface: An interface that allows you to have several documents or document views open at the same time. Also called *multiple design interface*.

N

natural end: A type of coil end that occurs as the natural result of the pitch, revolution, height, and profile of the coil.

network: Several ribs or webs created using the same direction and thickness.

neutral axis: The axis of a bend radius where neither stretching nor compressing occurs.

nominal size: The designated size of a commercial product.

nominal value: The value of a commercial product; intended to be the true drawn size without any specified limits.

O

oblique view: A 3D view in which the plane of projection is parallel to the front surface, and a receding angle is applied.

offset: Form objects parallel to the specified geometry at a specified distance apart. When referring to the

Thicken/Offset
tool, the process of offsetting a surface from a face or surface, similar to offsetting a work plane from a face. When referring to threads, the distance from the edge of the face to the beginning of threads.

open loop: A sketch that includes a gap(s) between objects.

open sketch profile: A sketch profile that does not form a closed loop.

ordinate dimensioning: A dimensioning method that provides coordinates from established datums that are usually located at the corner of the part or the axis of a feature. Also called *rectangular coordinate dimensioning without dimension lines* or *arrowless dimensioning*.

origin: The center point (0,0,0) of the model's XYZ coordinate system.

orphaned annotations: Annotations that have been moved away from a drawing view associated with model geometry.

orthographic view: A 2D view, or projection, in which the line of sight is perpendicular to a surface, such as the front of an object or the XY plane.

over-constrained model: A model with too many constraints.

P

pan: Reposition the display of objects in the graphics window.

panel bar: A panel-like window that appears by default on the left side of the Inventor graphics window. Panel bars are the primary default location for accessing design tools.

parallel: A geometric construction that specifies that objects such as lines and ellipse axes will never intersect, no matter how long they become.

parameters: Characteristics that control the size, shape, and position of model geometry. Shape and size limits placed on sketches and features.

parametric solid modeling: A form of modeling in which parameters and constraints drive the model form and function to produce models that contain object volume and mass data that can be used to analyze internal and external object characteristics.

parent node: An item in the tree structure, similar to a folder, that is associated with subordinate child nodes.

part: An item or product or an element of an assembly.

partial auxiliary view: An auxiliary view that shows the true size and shape of only the inclined surface, eliminating any projected geometry that may be foreshortened.

parts list: A table that records and displays the parts and subassemblies used to create an assembly.

path: A guide, or route, for creating sketched features.

pattern occurrences: Representations of patterned features that identify how many features are present because of the pattern operation.

perpendicular: A geometric construction that defines a 90° angle between objects such as lines and ellipse axes.

pitch: The distance parallel to the axis between a point on one coil spiral to the corresponding point on the next coil spiral. (Ch. 5) The distance parallel to the axis from a point on one thread to the corresponding point on the next thread.

pivot point: The point that acts as the center point when you are viewing and rotating model space objects.

placed features: Features added to an existing feature without using a sketch.

placed sections: Loft sections that are created without a sketch and are placed along a selected centerline. Placed sections are calculated based on the loft cross section at the selected location.

profile: The side or section outline of a sketched feature.

projects: Files that manage and organize folders and files for specific design jobs.

promote: Add to the part environment. Remove parts from a subassembly and make them individual parts in the parent assembly.

pull direction: The direction in which the casting mold is pulled or removed from the part.

pull-down menus: A text-based menu input system in which menu items appear when you pick the menu name.

punch: A press or similar tool used to form a specific shape or hole in sheet metal. Also called a *sheet metal punch*.

Q

quilt: A set of combined surfaces.

R

radius: The distance from the center of a circle or arc to its circumference.

radius dimension: A dimension used to define the radius of an arc or circular feature.

rail: A 2D or 3D sketched curve that is used in conjunction with sections to manipulate and further control the loft shape.

read-only: A file open option that allows you to view a file, but not make changes to it.

realtime zooming: Zooming that can be viewed as it is performed.

rectangular coordinate dimensioning without dimension lines: A dimensioning method that provides coordinates from established datums that are usually located at the corner of the part or the axis of a feature. Also called *ordinate dimensioning* or *arrowless dimensioning*.

rectangular feature pattern: Occurrences of features copied and positioned a specified distance apart, in rows and columns.

rectangular pattern: An arrangement of copies of a feature into a designated number of rows and columns placed a specified distance apart.

regular polygon: A geometric shape with three or more sides, such as a triangle, square, or hexagon, with all sides being equal in length and symmetrical about a common center.

revision table: A table that records drawing changes; usually placed in the upper-right corner of the drawing. Also called a *revision* *history block* or *revision block*.

revision tag: A symbol that identifies the location at which the engineering change occurs. The tag corresponds to a specific entry in the revision table. Also called a *revision symbol*.

revolution: A feature created in a circular path around an axis; also called a *revolved feature*. In a coil, one complete spiral, or 360° loop.

revolved feature: A feature created in a circular path around an axis. Also known as a *revolution*.

rib: A closed section of material usually added to reinforce a part without adding excessive material or weight.

right-hand threads: Threads that move a right-hand threaded bolt forward in a clockwise direction

rounds: Rounded exterior corners; rounds remove material from corners. A curve placed on the exterior intersection of two or more faces, removing material from a feature.

S

scale factor: The amount of enlargement or reduction.

screen space: A space, or environment, in which the graphics window controls model display; the center is located at the center of the graphics window.

sculpt: The process of using intersecting surfaces to add or remove solid mass.

sections: Sketches and existing feature faces used to develop loft features. A view that splits a part along a cutting-plane line to expose the interior features of the part. Also called a *section view*.

section view: A view that splits a part along a cutting-plane line to expose the interior features of the part. Also called a *section*.

setback: Point at which a fillet or round on one edge begins to combine with a fillet or round of at least two other edges.

shared content: Files available on the Internet, such as bolts from a bolt manufacturer, or components accessible on an intranet system, such as standard parts that are used for developing assemblies. Also called *third-party content*.

sharing: Making a sketch available for additional features after it has been used to create a feature.

sheet formats: Predefined, multiview drawing sheet templates that contain a default border and title block for various standard sheet sizes.

sheet metal punch: A press or similar tool used to form a specific shape or hole in sheet metal. Also called a *punch*.

shell: An operation that removes material from a feature and creates a hollow space or opening.

shortcut keys: Keyboard key combinations that allow you to access predefined tools.

shortcut menus: Menus that allow access to tools and options by right-clicking anywhere in the graphics window or on an object or selection.

sketch: A 2D drawing that provides the profile and/or guide for developing a sketched feature.

sketch center points: Points used to define the location of center points for features that reference center points, such as holes and sheet metal punches.

sketched features: Features such as extrusions, revolutions, sweeps, lofts, and coils that are built from a sketch.

sketch helix: A winding spiral shape primarily used to create springs, detailed threads, and similar items.

sketch pattern: Multiple arranged copies, or a pattern, of sketch shapes.

sketch points: Points used for construction purposes to help you develop sketch geometry.

spacing: In patterning, the distance between occurrences based on the width of the selected features and the distance between
the copies.

specific notes: Notes that apply to a specific feature or features on the drawing. Also called *local notes*.

spline: A complex curve defined by control points along the curve.

split: A feature that removes a portion of a model or divides faces at a separation sketch or plane.

spotface: Similar to a counterbore, but shallower; typically applied when a flush surface is necessary, such as to hide a flat washer, or in casting applications.

standard: A set of styles and other general drawing preferences that has been agreed upon and recommended for use by an industry, government, military, or standardssetting organization.

steering wheels: Circular navigation tools that allow you to navigate around a model.

stitched: Two or more surfaces combined to form a single surface or quilt.
supplement)

style library: A folder, Design Data by default, that houses styles in XML file format.

subassembly: An assembly placed in a larger assembly, such as switch, or spring assembly; subassemblies may be used more than once in the final assembled product.

surface extrusion: A volume less shape that is primarily used for construction purposes, allowing you to generate advanced models.

surface finish: The allowable roughness, waviness, lay, and flaws on a surface.

sweep: A feature created by guiding, or sweeping, a sketch profile along a sketch path.

T

table-driven iFeature: An iFeature that allows you to create multiple variations of the original iFeature using information stored in a spreadsheet.

tabular dimensioning: A type of arrowless dimensioning in which coordinate dimensions and size dimensions are given in a table that correlates with features on the drawing with a hole tag.

tangent constraint: A geometric construction that specifies how a curve touches another curve at the point of tangency.

tap: Use a machine tool to form an interior thread.

tapered threads: Threads often used for pipe fittings when a liquid or airtight seal is required.

templates: Files with predefined settings used to begin new documents.

thickening: The process of adding a solid to a face or surface, similar to a solid extrusion.

third-party content: Files available on the Internet, such as bolts from a bolt manufacturer, or components accessible on an intranet system, such as standard parts that are used for developing assemblies. Also called *shared content*.

thread class: The designated amount, or grade, of tolerance specified for the thread, ranging from fine to coarse threads.

threads: Grooves cut in a spiral fashion in or around the face of a cylindrical or conical feature.

title block: An area on the drawing sheet that contains information about the model, company, drafter, tolerances, and other design information.

tolerance stack: Text that is stacked horizontally without a fraction bar.

tool buttons: Buttons in a toolbar, each with a specific icon, that activate a tool or option.

tooltip: A small text box that displays when you hover over a button, giving information about the function of the button.

trails: Connection graphics between components that show their relative positions in the assembly.

transitional constraints: Constraints that identify relationships between the transitioning path of a fixed component and a component moving along the path.

transition angle: The number of degrees a coil end travels, or transitions, with pitch.

tweaks: Component modifications made during the preparation of a presentation.

U

under-constrained model: A model with elements that are unclear, can be changed or moved, or remain undefined.

user interface: The tools and techniques used to provide information to and receive information from a computer application. Also called an *interface*.

user parameters: Additional parameters defined by the user.

V

variable fillets and rounds: Fillets and rounds that have different curved radii placed at precise points between the start and end of a feature edge.

vertex: When referring to filet and round setbacks, the intersection of three or more edges.

virtual component: An assembly component used primarily to define a separate bill of materials item, without creating a model.

void: Any set of internal feature faces that define a hollow area in a solid.

W

walk-through: A viewing process that shows how it would look if you could walk in and around the actual product you are modeling.

web: An open section of material usually added to reinforce a part without adding excessive material or weight.

wedges: The parts of a steering wheel that contain navigation tools.

weldment: An assembly in which parts are fixed together with welds.

wireframe model: A model that contains only information about model edges and the intersection of edges.

wireframe representation: A display in which surfaces are removed so that you can see the edges clearly.

work axis: An axis used to create construction lines and axes. A parametric reference line that can be located anywhere in space.

work features: Features that direct the location and arrangement of other features. Construction points, lines, and surfaces that create reference elements anywhere in space to help position and generate additional features.

work planes: Planes that are used to create construction planes. Flat reference surfaces that can be located anywhere in space.

work points: Points used to create construction points. Parametric reference points that can be located on any part feature or in 3D space.

workspace: The default folder where files are located in a project.

Z

zoom in: Increase the displayed size of objects in the graphics window to view a smaller portion of the model, but in greater detail.

zoom out: Reduce the displayed size of objects in the graphics window to display more of the model, but in view less detail.

www.ingramcontent.com/pod-product-compliance
Lightning Source LLC
Chambersburg PA
CBHW081817300426
44116CB00014B/2400